Assessing Adolescents

Pergamon Titles of Related Interest

Apter/Goldstein YOUTH VIOLENCE: Programs and Prospects

Feindler/Ecton ADOLESCENT ANGER CONTROL:
Cognitive-Behavioral Techniques

Liebert/Sprafkin THE EARLY WINDOW: Effects of Television
on Children and Youth, Third Edition

Pope/McHale/Craighead SELF-ESTEEM ENHANCEMENT WITH
CHILDREN AND ADOLESCENTS

Rhodes/Jason PREVENTING SUBSTANCE ABUSE
AMONG CHILDREN AND ADOLESCENTS

Van Hasselt/Hersen HANDBOOK OF
ADOLESCENT PSYCHOLOGY

Related Journals *

CLINICAL PSYCHOLOGY REVIEW

JOURNAL OF CHILD PSYCHOLOGY AND PSYCHIATRY
AND ALLIED DISCIPLINES

JOURNAL OF SCHOOL PSYCHOLOGY

*Free sample copies available upon request

PSYCHOLOGY PRACTITIONER GUIDEBOOKS

EDITORS

Arnold P. Goldstein, Syracuse University
Leonard Krasner, Stanford University & SUNY at Stony Brook
Sol L. Garfield, Washington University in St. Louis

Assessing Adolescents

GERALD D. OSTER
JANICE E. CARO
DANIEL R. EAGEN
MARGARET A. LILLO

Regional Institute for Children and Adolescents
Rockville, MD

PERGAMON PRESS
New York · Oxford · Beijing · Frankfurt
São Paulo · Sydney · Tokyo · Toronto

U.S.A.	Pergamon Press, Inc., Maxwell House, Fairview Park, Elmsford, New York 10523, U.S.A.
U.K.	Pergamon Press plc, Headington Hill Hall, Oxford OX3 0BW, England
PEOPLE'S REPUBLIC OF CHINA	Pergamon Press, Room 4037, Qianmen Hotel, Beijing, People's Republic of China
FEDERAL REPUBLIC OF GERMANY	Pergamon Press GmbH, Hammerweg 6, D-6242 Kronberg, Federal Republic of Germany
BRAZIL	Pergamon Editora Ltda, Rua Eça de Queiros, 346, CEP 04011, Paraiso, São Paulo, Brazil
AUSTRALIA	Pergamon Press Australia Pty Ltd., P.O. Box 544, Potts Point, N.S.W. 2011, Australia
JAPAN	Pergamon Press, 5th Floor, Matsuoka Central Building, 1-7-1 Nishishinjuku, Shinjuku-ku, Tokyo 160, Japan
CANADA	Pergamon Press Canada Ltd., Suite No. 271, 253 College Street, Toronto, Ontario, Canada M5T 1R5

Copyright © 1988 Pergamon Press, Inc.

First edition 1988

Library of Congress Cataloging-in-Publication Data
Assessing adolescents/Gerald D. Oster . . . [et al.].
    p. cm. – (Psychology practitioner guidebooks)
    Includes index.
    ISBN 0-08-034941-2: $22.50.   ISBN 0-08-034940-4 (pbk.):
    $12.95
    1. Clinical child psychology.   2. Psychodiagnostics.
    3. Psychological tests for children.   4. Adolescent
    psychology.
    I. Oster, Gerald D.   II. Series.
    [DNLM: 1. Adolescent Psychology.   2. Psychological
    Tests – in adolescence.   3. Psychological Tests –
    methods.   WS 462 A846]
    RJ503.3.A77 1988   616.89'022–dc19
    DNLM/DLC

British Library Cataloguing in Publication Data
Assessing adolescents. — (Psychology
practitioner guidebooks).
1. Adolescents. Psychological assessment
I. Oster, Gerald D.   II. Series
155.5

ISBN 0-08-034941-2 (Hardcover)
ISBN 0-08-034940-4 (Flexicover)

Printed in Great Britain by A. Wheaton & Co., Ltd., Exeter

Contents

Foreword

Over the past fifteen years there have been remarkable advances in assessment techniques. New measures have been developed and disseminated; the administration, scoring and interpretation of traditional measures have been refined; and computer technology has entered the clinician's armamentarium. It is often difficult for the practicing clinician to keep abreast of these many advances. At the same time, the graduate student, confronted by the broad range of assessment measures available, often requires a comprehensive, yet concise, overview.

Assessing Adolescents is of great assistance to the experienced clinician wishing to enhance clinical skills, and to the clinical student beginning to develop clinical practices. The range of newer and traditional assessment measures presented include cognitive, educational, and neuropsychological assessments, personality inventories and behavior-based checklists, projective tests, and computerized assessment. In addition, the assessment process itself is discussed, from clarifying the referral questions through presenting written reports and interpretive sessions.

For newer psychological tests (e.g. the Personality Inventory for Children) or complex recent approaches to classic tests (e.g. the Exner Comprehensive System for the Rorschach), sufficient information regarding administration, scoring and psychometric properties is presented to enable the clinician to determine whether to consider incorporating these approaches into practice. References are provided for further exploration. In some instance (e.g. presentation of the formula for computation of deviation quotients for factors of the WISC-R), the clinician is provided with techniques that can be incorporated into practice immediately. Interview techniques, including the mental status examination, are described in a manner which enable beginning and advanced clinicians to check the thoroughness and sensitivity of their own techniques.

As both an educational and continuing educational tool, *Assessing Adolescents* is a valuable resource for clinicians working with adolescents.

Sandra R. Leichtman, Ph.D.
Chief Psychologist
State of Maryland
Mental Hygiene Administration
Baltimore, Maryland

Preface

The children now love luxury; they show disrespect for their parents, chatter before company, gobble up dainties at the table, and tyrannize over their teachers.

Socrates circa 420 B.C.

There is a considerable amount of interest within the physical and mental health professions regarding the behavioral and emotional problems of adolescents. Attention to this transitional stage between childhood and adulthood has brought together numerous theoreticians, researchers, and clinicians across several disciplines to grapple with problems of assessment, diagnosis, and treatment of the various disorders being presented by today's teenagers. Because of this renewed emphasis in identifying problem areas unique to this age group, psychologists and other professionals are constantly updating many formal and informal assessment devices. It is therefore, essential to stay abreast of the field, in order to have access to the important psychological information that is constantly being disseminated and to gain the crucial interviewing and relating skills necessary for work with adolescents and their families.

As three psychologists, who conduct psychological testing and supervise graduate students in this undertaking, and an audiologist who specializes in auditory information processing evaluations, the authors of this book find it is not only essential to become familiar with the strengths and weaknesses of certain tests or test batteries, it is equally important to provide accurate interpretations of the test data to families, juvenile justice officials, special education teachers, and those clinicians who will be directly treating the adolescent. In order to accomplish this, the examiner must be aware of the normative data and psychometric properties of the tests, consider the developmental level of the youth within the context of his/her background, and possess sound clinical judgment. In providing feedback to the referral sources, whether in written or oral form, the information must be presented clearly and in such a manner as to minimize distortions or the possibility of improper conclusions. Above all, the information must be relevant or it will be of little use to the profesionals involved in treatment.

Because of their unique knowledge about test construction and measurement, psychologists have been at the forefront in the development of a wide range of tests that attempt to tap various aspects of adaptive functioning. These include tests of intellectual and educational attainment; perceptual, motor, and language development; behavioral manifestations; and personality and emotional functioning. The range of these techniques is enormous, and has recently expanded to include an emphasis on brain–behavior relationships and on efficient administrative and interpretive strategies in the form of computerized assessment.

This book approaches the evaluation of adolescents from a broad perspective. Included is an overview of the most widely used psychological tests as well as practical strategies for interviewing adolescents and their families. Its purpose is also to emphasize the importance of communicating the results of these tests in a format that is understandable to the parties involved in the process. We have endeavored to create a practical and clinically-oriented guidebook that will provide to the practitioner: (a) an understanding of the dynamics surrounding the period of adolescence; (b) the skills required for conducting effective interviews; (c) a review of the psychometric instruments that have been widely used in the assessment of adolescents and some new developments in the field; (d) a look at the use of computers in the assessment process; and (e) tips on writing psychological reports and communicating the findings to families.

While the main readership for this guidebook is understood to be psychologists involved in the evaluation of adolescents and psychological examiners-in-training, other professionals and students, in various disciplines, who work with adolescents — such as pediatricians, child psychiatrists, social workers, nurses, diagnostic and prescriptive teachers, and allied health personnel — may also find the book a useful guide, to help them enlarge their own perspectives of the kinds of information psychologists can provide.

Chapter 1

Adolescents Within The Mental Health System

ADOLESCENCE: A NORMATIVE CRISIS

The period of adolescence is exciting and creative, yet it can be tumultuous and volatile. There are a considerable number of developmental hurdles that challenge the emotional and physical stability of adolescents themselves and also those who are in charge of their care, such as their family and the community system. Tasks that must be confronted include acceptance of bodily change, identity clarification, responsible sexuality, and coping with separations such as leaving home and the approach of adulthood. Additional areas for potential conflict are strong desires for group acceptance and subsequent peer pressures, initial exposure to drugs and alcohol, and concerns about school achievement, to name but a few. Concomitantly, changes in the family structure (e.g., death or divorce) can have an enormous impact on successful transition into adulthood, as can other familial circumstances such as socioeconomic status or frequent moves to different localities.

Blos (1962) has attempted to define the period of adolescence as adjusting psychologically to the condition of pubescence. Accordingly, he theorized that adolescents are heavily influenced by the physical alterations that occur, and, in turn, that these bodily changes impact more subtly on the adolescent's interpersonal relations, choice of interests, and emotional experiences. Within this interactional approach, Blos views the milieu and the adolescent's personal history as major forces influencing this phase of development.

By comparison, Erikson (1968) views adolescence from a perspective of normative crisis. During this segment of the life cycle, according to Erikson, there seem to be dramatic fluctuations in the adolescent's ego strength. The

1

primary resolution for this period is what Erikson has termed identity formation. Many of the major influencing factors involve psychosocial stress between the development of self and societal constraints. These interwoven themes, combining personal developmental issues with social requirements, are considered within the framework of the overriding historical time stage.

More recent theorists have maintained that it is impossible to study, assess, and treat adolescents without viewing the problem(s) in the context of the family system (Haley, 1973, 1980; Minuchin, 1974; Watzlawick, 1984). Mental health practitioners have found that effective assessment and treatment of adolescents in crisis can only occur when a full understanding of the family's history and dynamics are made clear. Within this framework, the presenting problems can be viewed as a signal that the entire family is "stuck", or in stress, in its attempt to move along their developmental path. The goal for the examiner then becomes to collect enough data on the adolescent and the family for effective treatment to occur.

REASONS FOR ADOLESCENT REFERRALS

Referrals for psychological testing can come from a variety of sources, including physicians (usually pediatricians or psychiatrists), juvenile justice representatives (judges, lawyers, or probation officers), and mental health professionals (e.g., social workers). Underlying the referral is the referring professional's need for additional information that would clarify diagnostic decisions, recommend treatment services, and/or measure treatment progress. Referrals are also made by educational officials and sometimes even directly by families, due to the presence of disruptive behaviors in school and in the home.

THE PSYCHOLOGIST'S ROLE IN THE REFERRAL QUESTIONS

The first step in assessing adolescents is to clearly delineate referral questions and clarify any probable expectations of the testing process by the referral source. When working within a multidisciplinary setting and/or system, there is usually a high degree of variability in sophistication regarding knowledge of child development, experience with severe psychopathology, and a general awareness of capabilities and limitations of psychological testing. Referrals often come to the examining psychologist in vague terms, underscoring the confusion surrounding both the presenting behavior of the adolescent and the benefits of psychological testing. Professionals or lay persons making referrals often have multiple or vague questions in mind that may not lend themselves to being directly addressed through the assessment process. For example, a frustrated parent or teacher may want the psychologist to discover possible explanations for a child's lack of motivation in school. This is an all-encompassing question, which is not specifically addressed in the most common assessment instruments. A more useful question, after obtaining further clarification from the referral source, may be: "Is the child's lack of progress in school part of a depressive process, low self-esteem, or a learning disability?" In order to gain the maximum benefit from an adolescent protocol, it is incumbent on the evaluator to question the referring agent so as to clearly pinpoint assessment objectives; then the evaluation process can be geared toward providing the referral source with appropriate conclusions.

Besides having the responsibility of clarifying the referral questions, the examining psychologist needs to have developed a certain degree of sophistication concerning the setting from which the referral has originated (Levine, 1981). It may mean learning another technical language, having an appreciation for the variety of roles of individuals working within a particular setting, and understanding the alternatives that confront those responsible for making crucial decisions or the different philosophical assumptions and beliefs of the individuals making the referral requests (Groth-Marnat, 1984). Both the issues behind the questions being asked and the information that can be derived from psychological assessment are complex, and it is imperative for the psychologist to be sure how the answers she or he gives will be used and disseminated. It is crucial to be aware that others' lives will somehow be affected by the findings from the test and interview data, and the way in which these are presented to the referral source will determine the effectiveness of the service to the adolescent and his or her family.

Psychologists engaged in the assessment of adolescents are aided by referral sources who supply clear, concise, and direct statements, verbally or in writing, regarding why a particular youth is being referred, what is known about this person (and family), and — of special importance — what expectations does the referral source have concerning the psychologist and the results of the assessment (Gabel, Oster, and Butnik, 1986). It needs to be emphasized that the responsibility for gathering this information clearly lies with the psychologist receiving the referral. It is especially important for the examining psychologist to aid the referral source in organizing his or her questions in such a manner as to specify which issues can readily be answered by testing and which are beyond the scope of psychological assessment. The examining psychologist should attempt to understand the choices confronted by the referral person (e.g., should a judge order a 14-year-old emotionally disturbed boy who is a repeat delinquent to be sent to a residential psychiatric treatment center as opposed to a detention center), in addition to the possible alternatives within the system and the degree to which each alternative may be useful to a particular youth.

Specific information to be solicited from the referral sources should include the following:

1. What is the nature of the presenting problem as understood by the referral source? (If a family is requesting a psychological evaluation, what is their main complaint?)
2. At what stage in the contact with the referral source is this request for psychological assistance being made? (e.g., the pediatrician has known a 14-year-old since childhood, or an assessment is being requested from a primary therapist to determine gains made after six months in therapy).
3. What prior testings have been completed? Often psychologists will receive referrals for testing when thorough evaluations have already been completed within the recent past. It is essential to request from the referral source all known past evaluations. It is also important for the psychologist to make some phone calls to schools and physicians who have had contact with this youth, in order to identify which additional information is needed for effective treatment and to secure their input. Not only do tests become invalid when given frequently, but it is a waste of valuable time and money to retest a youth when this information is already known.
4. What is going to be the role of the psychologist after the assessment is completed? Will the psychologist be expected to inform the parents and the youth of the testing results? Is the assessing psychologist expected to take on the case in therapy?
5. What other information might benefit you as the psychologist performing a particular evaluation (e.g., a history of family pathology, current stressors on the family)?

COMMON REFERRAL SOURCES

Pediatricians

A pediatrician is the primary care physician of children and adolescents and in this capacity usually has an abundance of information to offer a psychologist in regard to past history, health concerns, and hypotheses relating to the cognitive or emotional disorder of an identified youth. A pediatrician may refer for psychological testing in the treatment of attention deficit disorder, for example, when a stimulant medication is being prescribed and a baseline of test data is required to determine effectiveness, or may do so when learning problems are encountered after early successes and questions are being raised about the possibility of emotional problems or a specific learning disability that is hindering intellectual growth. Nowadays, the pediatrician will often find him or herself involved in the coordination of, in collaboration with psychologists and educators, the treatment of severe emotional disturbance, such as eating disorders. Therefore, the pediatrician will almost assuredly be placed in the role of requesting psychological testing on at least some occasion (Gabel, Oster, and Butnik, 1986).

When receiving a referral from a pediatrician, it is essential to discover what assessment instruments have already been used (many pediatricians are comfortable using intellectual screening tests such as the Peabody Picture Vocabulary Test and behavioral rating forms such as the Child Behavior Checklist) in order to provide supportive or supplemental information. It is also valuable to discover what other tests have already been ordered by the pediatrician (e.g., a CAT scan), regardless of the outcome of the psychological testing. Also pediatricians usually have comprehensive psychosocial and medical histories and can provide interesting data of early trauma and how it may have contributed to the current problems in behavior. Finally, it is essential to discover early in the referral whether or not the pediatrician will deliver the results of the testing to the parents and what future role the pediatrician will want the psychologist to perform (e.g., as the primary therapist).

Psychiatrists

Psychiatrists are found in a wide variety of roles within the mental health system, and within these roles have distinct responsibilities in the diagnosis, treatment, and management of disturbed adolescents. For example, they can be seen as unit chiefs in psychiatric hospitals, as consultants to treatment teams, or as independent practitioners. In each of these roles, they face different problems for which psychological testing can be a valuable asset. Such issues as potential for suicide, admission and discharge decisions, and assessing the degree of reality testing in an individual are common problems that confront the psychiatrist. Thus, the referral for psychological testing from the psychiatrist often involves questions such as degree of ego strength, depth of depression, and presence of disorganized thinking.

Testing protocols assist psychiatrists to gather comprehensive data on which to base decisions concerning such matters as placement within or outside of a hospital or treatment center, what other testings are needed to rule out various pathologies, and what therapies, if any, could best help a particular youth. An ambiguous request for "a psychological" is meaningless, even when the psychologist has some preconceived notion as to the information needed; therefore, psychologists must urge the referring psychiatrist to be specific in terms of desired information. A dialogue between the psychologist and psychiatrist — in which the former educates on specifics of psychological testing, given the particular presenting questions, and the latter educates on the specific individual being referred — will be most beneficial in providing pertinent and useful data.

AA—B

Educators

As when working with physicians, the psychologist who is either employed within the school system or who is consulting to special educators must familiarize him or herself with the way educators conceptualize the myriad problems presented by adolescents. For example, the term "specific learning disabilities" may be used differently by teachers, who may be concerned that "Johnny cannot read," than by administrators, who may be concerned only with a primary diagnosis for placement. Being aware of the number and types of available resources is of utmost importance, so that one can effectively make knowledgeable recommendations to educational referral sources. Without a clear knowledge of the context within which the psychological evaluation is being conducted, it is likely that the examining psychologist will not provide substantive feedback to the people who are requesting his or her trained input (Groth-Marnat, 1984).

The primary focus of the schools is to find an appropriate placement for each student who is being educated. Under Public Law 94-142, it is the responsibility of the school system to provide both the assessment of children manifesting learning and behavior problems and appropriate classroom alternatives. Therefore, the majority of testing referrals stem from the need to abide by this law, which requires frequent reevaluation (at least once every three years).

Focusing only on the student's strengths and weaknesses may blind the system to the larger social context. Factors such as family dysfunction and interpersonal stress are likely to have a major influence on learning style, but may not be reflected by the requested assessment. Although gaining access to this broader base of information can provide a more accurate picture of the learning problem, it may create significant complications as to the legal and ethical right of the school to delve into personal family information. Thus, the psychologist receiving referrals from educators must be sensitive to the fact that her or his basic assumptions for the purposes of testing may differ from the way in which the results will actually be used, and to address these issues in the recommendations.

Juvenile Justice Officials

The psychologist in the juvenile court system will usually make treatment recommendations based upon the psychological profile of the youth being examined. One of the basic questions to be answered by the juvenile judge is to decide on proper in- or outpatient treatment. The overriding referral question in juvenile court then becomes, the degree of required structure necessary for a particular youth to receive treatment. That is, will the youth on trial require a structured or semi-structured living arrangement, and, if so, what are the best alternatives? Perhaps the youth on trial will only need to live by ground rules at home, rules that can be established by the court and his or her probation officer, and can therefore, return to the family. Another youth may be more in conflict with society's rules and regulations, and will require a more structured setting in which to maximize the benefits of his or her treatment. An additional question is whether this particular youth will derive benefits from psychotherapy, and it is the psychological examiner's responsibility to determine which therapeutic modality would likely be most effective, e.g., individual, family or group therapy. Finally, some determination of why this person is acting out at this particular time (i.e., Is this adolescent depressed? Is he or she reacting to a recent trauma? Was this an isolated incident or a pattern of coping to stress?) is relevant to the formulation of sentencing and needs to be assessed.

The general decisionmaking approach of the legal system is often counter to the training of a psychologist. From the standpoint of an attorney (all adolescents are allowed legal representation), each case is unique to the individual and the circumstances. To a psychologist who has been trained to create generalizations (Cowan, 1963), this presents a dilemma. The examining psychologist is requested to provide data from which inferences concerning daily functioning can be made. The inferences must stand up to precise questioning and examination, relying heavily on the supportive psychological data. The psychologist doing court evaluations must be sensitive to these demands and needs to have a clear understanding regarding the questions being asked and the reasons. The ultimate decisionmaker, i.e., the juvenile court judge, does indeed place much emphasis on the psychological report.

Primary Therapists

Primary therapists of adolescents usually request a psychological evaluation at a point of change in treatment. This may include gaining information about their client's cognitive and emotional resources when beginning therapy, in order to clarify treatment goals and to plan appropriate treatment strategies, or prior to transfer to another agency (e.g., a youth leaving a residential treatment center who will be seen at the local mental health clinic), in order to provide the next therapist with a clearer understanding of the dynamics that may still be impacting on the youth's progress. Standard questions from primary therapists may involve identifying relevant psychosocial stressors and formulating descriptions of personality, including defense mechanisms, cognitive and learning styles, capacity for insight, range of affect, and current diagnoses.

Referral questions from the primary therapist may initially be vague and it will be worth the psychologist's time to talk to the therapist and help him or her reformulate the referral questions and specify goals for the testing. The primary therapists have valuable knowledge of the underlying dynamics and the interpersonal style of their teenage clients, as well as the wider scope of family and social agency involvement. When assisting with the reformulation of the referral questions during the middle of treatment, the psychologist may help the primary therapist discover that therapy is "stuck" and the therapist is really looking for another avenue in which to address the client. In these cases, the psychological examiner may want to explore other issues with the primary therapist — for instance, possibly unrealistic expectations for change or countertransferance issues — that may impede progress and may be more relevant than a (test-generated) description of the youth's personal characteristics (Groth-Marnat, 1984).

Families

When referrals for psychological testing come from families, the parents are usually already frustrated by the stress involved in dealing with the countless problems encountered by their adolescent child, and are desperate for something to change. Often families contact psychologists at the request of other agency personnel due to the strain that their child has placed on the social system, most commonly the school. In receiving these referrals, it is important to clarify the family's reasons for the testing and their expectations of the outcome — that is, what do they anticipate the testing will accomplish?

It is paramount for the psychologist to have a clear understanding of the youth's social network and all the reasons for the particular referral (Groth-Marnat, 1984). A complete history should be gathered of previous strategies used in working with this child and what has and has not been effective. Information concerning prior treatment and the attitudes among the parents and the other components of the social system is essential. Without an accurate understanding of the context of the referral, the psychologist might find him or herself in the middle of a larger entanglement that would not benefit anyone involved in the situation.

It is typical that referral of an adolescent by a family only comes after a long sequence of events, and it is incumbent upon the evaluator to obtain details of all these precipitants. After ascertaining the family's view of the situation and their reasons for initiating an evaluation of their child, the examiner should clarify any questions that may be lingering with other sources in the child's network, including school personnel, lawyers, probations officers, and other therapists. A direct meeting with these individuals is always desirable and well worth the time spent, as the meetings are usually extremely valuable for effective treatment planning. The alert examiner must realize that the family's decision to request an evaluation of their child is not an isolated event and there are typically many important decisions to be made based on the results of the testing. The matters to be decided may include special education interventions, custody changes, and inclusion in various therapies.

DISORDERS OF ADOLESCENCE

Learning Disabilities

It is important to identify the existence of learning disabilities in adolescents, since one cannot assume that all learning disabilities have been identified in early childhood nor that they have been adequately addressed. Adolescents with a history of difficulties in any of the perceptual, integrative, memory, or expressive functions required in the learning process will have most likely developed a number of compensatory strategies for coping with their disability(ies).

Unfortunately, not all strategies provide socially acceptable behaviors. For example, adolescents who have learned to shut out all incoming stimuli in an effort to minimize confusion when they feel overwhelmed with a given task may begin to act out their feelings. These youths may have developed high frustration levels; have poor self images; be physically exhausted by the end of a school day; see themselvs as failures, because they cannot remember the explanations or directions necessary to complete assignments; be irritable; or may have high stress and tension levels. All these symptoms, experienced due to underlying sensory problems or learning difficulties, make these youths prime candidates for the expression of disruptive behavior and emotional problems.

Conditions classified as learning disabilities include, among others: dyslexia, dysgraphia, developmental arithmetic difficulties, developmental language problems, developmental articulation dysfunction, perceptual handicaps, and neurological impairments (McCarthy & McCarthy, 1969). The group of children that are labeled and diagnosed as *Learning Disabled* (LD) are not a homogeneous group. Various psychological and educational deficits are included by this "umbrella" term.

Although a great number and variety of definitions for Learning Disability exist, an adequate definition should specify that these children:

1. manifest an educationally significant discrepancy between their estimated intellectual potential and actual level of performance (two years below grade level);
2. have deficits related to basic disorders in the learning process;
3. may or may not have accompanied central nervous system dysfunction;
4. experience learning disabilities that are *not* secondary to generalized mental retardation, educational or cultural derivation, severe emotional disturbance, or sensory loss (Myers & Hammill, 1969).

The characteristics of the learning disabled youth are generally considered to be either the reasons for or the results of the learning disability. The only common trait to be found among adolescents with learning difficulties is a discrepancy between apparent ability to learn and actual academic achievement. Adolescents may have one or more of the following characteristics:

Hyperactivity

Short Attention Span

Visual Perceptual Disorders
- Reversal of letters and numbers
- Inadequate reproduction of geometric designs
- Poor handwriting

Auditory Perceptual Disorders
- Poor discrimination between gross sounds or speech sounds
- Difficulty separating or centering on target sounds in a noisy background

Motor Problems —
- Clumsiness or awkwardness
- Poor motor coordination

Memory Disorders
- Inability to acquire and retain information
- Difficulty remembering sequential information
- Inability to repeat sentences

Language Disorders
- Inability to internalize and organize experiences to provide a basis for later spoken or written language
- Expressive language difficulties (oral or written)
- Receptive language problems (oral or written)
- Auditory closure disorders
- Coding problems

Disruptive Behaviors

Probably the most common referrals of adolescents for psychological evaluations are those youths who have been socially disruptive and have been targeted for intervention since early in their school careers. The defining characteristics of this subgroup of adolescents are aggressive behaviors, resistance to discipline, destructiveness, impulsivity, high levels of activity, and lapses in concentration (Stewart, 1980). In trying to define this subgroup of children into a distinct nosological classification, the revised Diagnostic and Statistical Manual of Mental Disorders (third edition) (DSM-III-R) (Spitzer & Williams, 1987) has grouped the previously separate diagnoses of Attention-deficit Hyperactivity Disorder, Conduct Disorder, and Oppositional Defiant Disorder into a single subclass of interpersonal problems described as Disruptive Behavior Disorders.

The main features of Attention-deficit Hyperactivity Disorder are age inappropriate lack of attention, impulsive behavior, and over-activity. In school, the adolescent who has difficulty sustaining attention will often fail to complete tasks or class assignments, will appear not to be listening to the teacher, and is usually easily distracted by peers or influences in the immediate environment. Features of impulsivity are typically seen by the youth who experiences difficulty in organizing his or her work, who often shouts out in class, and who needs much of the teacher's time and attention. Hyperactivity is evidenced by excessive activity (e.g., frequent running or climbing and fidgeting) and the inability to relate quietly. The most outstanding characteristics of this disorder in adolescents appear to be a general restlessness, careless performance of school-related tasks, and spurning interpersonal responsibility. In the majority of cases where hyperactivity persists into adolescence, conduct and oppositional behavior problems often develop.

When an adolescent displays a disruptive pattern of behavior which persists over time, serious consequences usually result. Repeated violations against persons and societal regulations force significant adults to take harsher actions; school suspension may occur, or the juvenile justice system may become involved. These officials want to know from the assessment whether actions of the teenager, such as physical aggression, stealing, constant lying, and/or chronic truancy or running away, have an emotional component that may respond to psychological intervention.

The associated features seen in this group of youngsters (for example, lack of remorse for their antisocial actions, blaming others for their behavior, poor frustration tolerance, academic underachievement, alcohol and drug abuse) tend to occur early in adolescence. The degree and intensity of actions against others or against rules and regulations may be seen as a predisposition towards a character disorder (e.g., Antisocial Personality Disorder) when the teenager becomes an adult.

When these negative and hostile behaviors are observed without the more serious violations against others, a diagnosis of Oppositional Defiant Disorder may be a more accurate description of the disorder (Spitzer & Williams, 1987). Behaviors such as temper outbursts, arguments against adult authority, frequent expressions of annoyance, and many expressions of anger are observed. It is only when these behaviors occur in excess of what would be deemed normal for this age group that a significant disturbance would be noted. Because these behaviors are generally limited to familiar situations and persons, these symptoms may not be evident during an evaluation; thus the need for corroborating evidence from family, teachers, and others familiar with the situation.

Emotional Disturbance

Many emotional problems of adolescents have anxiety and fear as the main feature. In adolescence, test anxiety, a common problem, may interfere with effective academic functioning, leading indirectly to impaired identity formation. School phobia can also interrupt educational attainment and interfere with normal growth and development. Fears connected with medical personnel or procedures could prevent the adolescent from receiving adequate health treatment. Other fears or anxieties may interfere with everyday functioning such as eating and sleeping, while others may block a youth from entering a building or driving a car. In order to formulate effective treatment plans, it is imperative to obtain during the clinical interview a detailed account of the situational contexts which accompany these anxious feelings.

Another source of emotional tension during the adolescent years is depressed symptoms, such as dysphoria, self-deprecating thoughts, and feelings of helplessness. Although less than 10 per cent of adolescents could be diagnosed as experiencing a major depression, many young people do exhibit tiredness and difficulties in concentration, and express somatic complaints (Weiner, 1980). When teenagers find themselves unable to verbalize these feelings, they are more likely to act them out through antisocial or delinquent behaviors, such as drug usage or sexual promiscuity. When these feelings become overwhelming, suicidal thoughts and gestures become a possibility. It is incumbent upon the psychological examiner to gauge the degree of depression in the individual being tested and determine whether active intervention is required if there is a chance of suicide.

Childhood psychosis represents a range of severe, pervasive disorders of intellectual, perceptual, and emotional functioning (Fish & Ritvo, 1979). The adolescent considered schizophrenic most often presents to the examiner as uninvolved, withdrawn, or emotionally aloof. The affected youth's comprehension of reality tends to be markedly distorted from the norm and there is likely to be evidence of visual–motor and overall movement deficits. Although psychotic youth may experience common features with other emotionally disturbed youngsters (e.g., anxiety), their experience tends to be more severe (e.g., panic attacks). It is important for the examiner to determine the range of disturbance in such areas as personal hygiene, school, and interpersonal relations and whether the onset has been since early childhood or a more recent phenomenon.

Personality Disorders

The diagnosis of personality disorders requires evidence of continuous maladaptive behavioral patterns, usually recognizable by adolescence

(Mishne, 1986). When these traits are seen in younger children they are generally seen as part of the developing child and are considered behavior disturbances that have as yet not been ingrained. Like children, teenagers are normally in a state of disequilibrium where their actions and tendencies are not fixed and integrated. Ultimately, at least three conditions are required in order to label an adolescent as experiencing a personality disorder. These include: (a) the presentation of definite behavioral aberrations; (b) a clearly formed and identifiable pattern of interpersonal relating; and (c) the absence of transient situations identified as the cause of the disturbance (Finch & Green, 1979).

For many clinicians, personality disorder connotes a static and fixed condition where prognosis is poor; thus, clinicians who are involved with children and adolescents are more reluctant to use these diagnostic entities (Meeks, 1979). Also, although many features of these disorders, such as Dependent or Borderline Personality Disorder, may be seen during episodes of acute stress, they may not be typical of long-term functioning. According to DSM-III-R, several adult Axis II categories have corresponding relationships to disorders in childhood and adolescence. For instance, Conduct Disorder is sometimes viewed as the precursor to Antisocial Personality Disorder, although research has indicated that not all children displaying antisocial behavior continue their actions into adulthood. Likewise, the Identity Disorder in adolescence shares many of the characteristics of the adult Borderline.

Adolescents can be viewed as having an already formed disturbance in personality functioning when they have attempted to resolve their internal stress by forming rigid patterns in reacting to their environment, often causing external conflict (Mishne, 1986). These fixed patterns of behavior allow the adolescent to receive at least partial gratification of instinctual wishes and rationalizations for their motives. Because these youngsters do not exhibit the pain or guilt of normal or slightly neurotic persons, they are less motivated to change their position. These are the teenagers whose behavior is disturbing to others and cause much concern to parents and teachers, and whose stance is stubborn and unyielding. They are also viewed as having little ability to cope with boredom, frustration, and aggression; they have distorted interpersonal relations, and a poor conception of reality (Redl & Wineman, 1951).

Because familial and contextual factors often play a large role in personality-disordered adolescents, and because their style of relating has been fixed for some time, treatment is clearly difficult and frustrating (Mishne, 1986). Much of the struggle that is seen in working with these youngsters is due at least in part to their superficial facade and their lack of genuine feelings. They often express little empathy towards others and have a difficult time accepting trusting relationships. Thus, they are left isolated due to their inability to engage in peer friendships and lack of meaningful ties with adults. Their inaccessibility many times leaves the clinician or worker involved with their care tired and angry.

Eating Disorders

Eating disorders that present during adolescence reflect complex and interrelated factors that stem from psychological, biological, behavioral, ethnic, and sociological sources of tension (Harkaway, 1987). Although the symptoms of such disturbances as obesity or anorexia nervosa may be obvious to the examiner or diagnostician, the formulation of effective treatment strategies becomes difficult when considering all the multiple components of the presenting problems.

Overweight teenagers may experience a low self-esteem, have episodes of depressive thoughts, and sense feelings of hopelessness about overcoming their problems. Although some researchers have concluded that inadequate knowledge about diet and poor eating habits are the primary problems of these groups of adolescents, others have pointed to the glaring lack of social and verbal skills in these youngsters (Saffer & Kelly, 1974). Since a direct therapeutic approach to behavioral change is often difficult in treating adolescents, many clinicians find it necessary to recommend individual and group therapies to enhance the feelings of self-worth and increase social participation.

Anorexia nervosa is a disorder consisting of excessive self-imposed restrictions in eating that generally begins during adolescence (Stein & Davis, 1982). Besides the extreme dieting, there can also be instances of overeating followed by vomiting. Its essential features include a weight loss of at least 25 per cent of normal body weight and the refusal to maintain a minimum of weight that would be considered within the norm for age and height. The vast majority of teenagers with this condition are females. Oftentimes the dieting is precipitated by fears of being overweight which may lead to a withdrawal from peers and immature behavior within the home situation. The family situation may include struggles over power and control with parents interfering with the progression towards increased maturity and independence. When encountering situations such as this, the examiner must conduct thorough and nonthreatening individual and family interviews in order to begin to reestablish normal eating patterns and promote healthy family interactions.

CONCLUDING REMARKS

Adolescents stand at the nexus between childhood and adulthood. Consequently, the psychologist must not only have an understanding of the developmental phases of adolescence, but must have an integral knowledge of the developmental processes of childhood from which the adolescent has emerged, as well as the stages of adulthood to which the adolescent is headed. Additionally, a broad understanding of pathological conditions in adolescents and their families is essential for the clinician interested in conducting comprehensive evaluations. Finally, an ability to relate to adolescents, to be open to many different forms of communication, and to be genuine in the assessment process itself will serve to maximize the information to be gathered.

In order to gain this needed information, several steps must be undertaken. These include: (a) interviewing the adolescent and conducting a mental status examination; (b) obtaining background information from the family and being able to view the adolescent's problems within the context of the family; and (c) administering psychological tests that portray the adolescent's strengths and weaknesses. The ultimate goal of the assessment process is then to delineate problem areas and to determine intervention strategies such that the adolescent can be assisted toward a more satisfactory level of adjustment. In order to guarantee success in this orientation, to provide real assistance toward correcting the problem areas, the clinician must be able to clearly present his or her findings in an understandable manner in both written and oral form. The remaining portions of this book will detail these essential steps in the comprehensive assessment of adolescents.

Chapter 2

Diagnostic Interviewing of Adolescents

THE INITIAL PHASE

Establishing Rapport

In order to effectively assess adolescents, clinicians must be well trained in conducting diagnostic interviews. Adolescents rarely refer themselves for treatment, and therefore are usually seen because of someone else's distress over their behavior, mood or attitude. Consequently the degree to which the adolescent will comply with the interview process may be quite variable. Contrastingly, adults, who usually have had a previous experience with being interviewed, are somewhat prepared in terms of what to expect and the role in the interview they will undertake. This same set of assumptions is not always true for the adolescent brought to a mental health facility. Therefore, in order to maximize the amount of information gathered and the utility of that information in terms of diagnosis and treatment planning, it is important that the clinician be sensitive to both the fact that adolescents are probably not coming on their own volition and that they are also probably confused and anxious as to the expectations and process of the interview itself.

Providing Structure

In order to decrease some of the probable anxieties, resistance, and misconceptions the adolescent brings to the first appointment, the clinician needs to be initially more active in providing a structured framework in the beginning phase of the interview. For instance, being prompt for the start of the interview can decrease nervousness and forestall any additional outpouring of anger (Weins & Matarazzo, 1983). Initiating the introduction process and directing the adolescent to a chair in the office can also assist in decreasing anxiety. Exchanging some social amenities, such as how the adolescent should address you and how she or he wants to be called, is also helpful (Weins & Matarazzo, 1983). Finally, a short description of the interview process itself, as well as some brief information about the adolescent which the clinician has already obtained from the referring source, should also be shared. Adolescents are generally wary of adults; therefore, introducing role expectations and offering straightforward communications of articulated problem areas can, in most cases, de-escalate anxiety and promote an atmosphere that can stimulate disclosure of personally relevant information on the part of the adolescent. The following case vignette illustrates the structuring process of the interview:

Dr. Smith: Hello, I'm Dr. Smith and you must be Kevin Jones. (pauses to shake Kevin's hand and get a response from Kevin).

Kevin: Hello.

Dr. Smith: Kevin, we are going to go into my office for a little while to talk ... Why don't you have a seat in this blue chair. Is Kevin the name you like to be called, or do you have a preferred nickname?

Kevin: Kevin is fine.

Dr. Smith: Well, Kevin, today we are going to spend a little while talking. I want to get a chance to get to know you. Your parents have brought you here today because they are concerned about your many absences from school and your failing grades. They also seem worried that you are "hanging around with the wrong crowd." So today I want to get your opinion of the situation — to ask you about school, your family, your friends, what kind of interests you have — and find out about the way you think. Are there any questions you have before we begin?

Kevin: Nope.

Dr. Smith: O.K., why don't we start by your telling me how you see things in reference to the problems your parents told me about?

Facing Shy Youngsters

With the above prompts, the adolescent will often begin to share some information about him or herself. However, the problem for clinicians is when this structuring of the interview process does not lead to a disclosure of relevant information. The shy adolescent may not be stimulated to begin to enumerate on problem areas even after the clinician has introduced the adolescent to the interview process. For the shy or confused youngster, starting the session by reviewing problem areas may be too intimidating. Instead, an initially less confrontational approach might be more advantageous. Questions regarding the adolescent's age, school grade, favorite academic subjects, favorite sports and hobbies, or favorite music group may allow him or her to feel more comfortable with the interview process and enhance the possibility of further personal disclosures. As the interviewer listens to the answers provided, she or he can begin to question in more depth the thoughts and feelings being expressed. By transmitting a sense of genuine interest and caring in the adolescent's situation, the clinician can be of assistance in creating an environment in which more withdrawn youngsters can begin to feel more comfortable in describing their concerns.

Confronting Anger

A real challenge for clinicians is presented by those adolescents who manifest a tremendous amount of anger and rage. These individuals are usually guarded and suspicious in their interactions with adults, thus frequently making interviewing a difficult process. Additionally, these youngsters are often brought to the interview under considerable duress. As their style is often to project their anger and anxiety outward, either through a belligerent attitude or through destructive behaviors, these adolescents usually have alienated those around them prior to being brought to mental health professionals. They usually only attend the interview because some great threat, imposed by their guardians, is "hanging over their heads." Once at the interview, they may view the clinician as an extension of that threat, and may offer little in the way of cooperation with the objectives of the interview process.

Strategies for Overcoming Resistance

There are, however, a number of strategies which can assist the clinician in countering even the best efforts of a belligerent and hostile youngster. First, the clinician should maintain an open mind despite information gained through the referral source concerning the adolescent's degree of hostility. Frequently, clinicians can become biased through referral information and may therefore expect youngsters to be hostile and resistant to the interview process. For example, parents can call soliciting help for their child, and tell the clinician over the phone that "they are unsure they can get the youngster to the interview and if they do he or she won't say a thing" or a clinician can learn prior to the interview about rather outlandish hostile behaviors in which the adolescent has engaged. Many times, when these adolescents actually come in for the appointment, they are engaging and willing to participate. If the clinician expects hostility and resistance, it may become a self-fulfilling prophesy. Although anger and aggression almost always have an interpersonal context, the processes that stimulate anger in the adolescent's home and school environment may not be operative in the evaluative session. However, if the clinician expects this hostility, she or he may be repeating the interactional patterns that exist in the adolescent's social environment.

Finally, adolescents who use a more guarded and aggressive style usually do so as a last resort, either to levy some control over anxiety or because they feel threatened by the external environment. This style is often not a preferred mode of interaction but one that has grown out of difficulties in adequately coping. Providing the expectation that adolescents will behave properly in an interview situation, the clinician can help create an environment where they can have the experience of more adaptive functioning, and can stimulate them to try more appropriate behaviors.

Engaging Hostile Youngsters

Even when entering the interview with an open mind, clinicians do at times face adolescents who present as extremely hostile and belligerent. These youths often deny any and all problems, and are quite inhibited in terms of revealing information about themselves. It is important in these instances to start with the adolescent's view of the referral source's or parent's concerns. For example, if the youngster denies any problems, a gentle but direct statement such as "Are your parents making this up?" usually produces dialogue about unfair or irrational parental expectations. This is important data and should not be discarded, even though the adolescent has not admitted behaviors well documented from a variety of sources. Once challenged, the resistant adolescent may be quite revealing of his or her opinions. If part of the rationale for conducting the interview is to obtain the adolescent's perspective, his or her opinion should be respected, even though it is presented in an aggressive and perhaps unrealistic manner.

If attempts made to engage these youngsters in a straight and forthright manner fail, there are some alternative strategies which can be employed to facilitate the interview process. These strategies usually entail highly confrontational statements and should be used only occasionally. For example, an adolescent who is extremely defiant may be engaged in the interview process by entering into a challenging situation with the examiner. This strategy is most useful with delinquent populations, in which the strive for autonomy is great and the level of noncompliance with — and distrust of — authority figures is also high. The following is a case vignette of this challenging style of interaction. In this dialogue, there is a subtle challenge being offered which feeds into the narcissism and need for control that these kinds of adolescents present to the interviewer. While it is not the preferred method for engaging an adolescent, it does have some utility in beginning the interview process when resistance is paramount.

Dr. Walters: John, your parents tell me that they have a lot of concerns about you, especially with regard to the recent juvenile charges you have incurred for theft.

John: They worry too much. I'd be a lot better off if they just left me alone, including not making me come to this stupid interview. I have nothing to say.

Dr. Walters: Can you tell me about your parents worrying?

John: No, I don't want to tell you anything.

Dr. Walters: John, you said your parents made you come to the interview. Are they always this successful at getting you to do what they want?

John: No, I am my own boss.

Dr. Walters: So you came willingly to the interview, perhaps you were curious about what this was all about?

Final Comments

In summary, the initial phase of the interview process should focus on introductions, establishing a relationship with the adolescent, and setting an atmosphere which encourages disclosures of personal and relevant information on the part of the adolescent. These objectives can only be reached if the clinician is able to meet the adolescent where she/he is and to be willing to allow for an unfolding of the youngster's thoughts and feelings: the clinician must be able to transmit a genuine sense of *interest* in the adolescent's thoughts and feelings. This can be facilitated by communicating directly to the adolescent that his or her perspective is important in gaining a comprehensive picture of the presenting situation. Toward this end, the clinician must be sensitive and respectful of the adolescent's ability to relate information. The adolescent is often brought to the interview with a pervasive sense of inadequacy and failure. The clinician who can communicate that she or he values what the adolescent has to offer in terms of reactions and opinions enhances both the interview process and the ability to devise appropriate strategies for intervention.

Clinicians must also be aware of their own manner of interacting in creating a conducive atmosphere. For example, clinicians who are overly friendly or who want to portray themselves as the client's "buddy," would probably decrease the amount of information obtained: adolescents would be suspicious because this is not a usual role adults play in their lives. Contrastingly, clinicians who present in a very distant and aloof manner, with no empathy, humor, or ability to demonstrate some relatedness to the adolescent's world, would have limited success gathering comprehensive information through the interview process. Additionally, the clinician who becomes defensive when confronted by adolescent challenges regarding the interviewer's motives for certain lines of questioning may also retard the interview process.

It is important to remember that few adolescents have experienced a formalized interview, and thus their curiosity about the process may not be just a manifestation of a guarded and suspicious style but may reflect more pronounced issues they have about themselves, what others think, and what will constitute the next step after the interview. It is best, when possible, to answer their questions concerning the interview process itself in a straight and forthright manner.

MIDDLE PHASE

Once the introductions have been accomplished and a rapport established with the adolescent, the focus of the interview shifts to gathering more specific information in order to formulate a diagnostic impression and develop a plan for intervention. While the clinician should be observant from the very inception of the interview concerning the adolescent's appearance, manner of relating, and content of verbalizations, it is during the middle phase of the interview that the clinician should concentrate more intently on making an assessment of the adolescent's functioning. This is accomplished through exploration of the adolescent's world (his or her thoughts and feelings with regard to home, school, and social environments) and through the Mental Status Exam (a formal assessment of the adolescent's behavior, speech, affect and mood, thought processes and content, memory, fund of knowledge, concentration, and judgment).

Being Flexible

In the middle phase of the interview, the clinician must strike a balance between active structuring of the interview process and allowing for more spontaneous interactions. By imposing some structure into the interview situation, the clinician can make an assessment of the adolescent's reaction to external demands and limits. Conversely, by giving the adolescent some freedom in the interview, the clinician allows the youngster to demonstrate a sample of his or her interpersonal relatedness. During this process, the clinician is making various hypotheses with regard to diagnostic inferences about the adolescent. By asking specific questions, some competing diagnostic entities can be largely ruled out. The clinician must make sure to ask specific questions, especially those centering around various clusters of symptoms, yet the interviewer must also be open to explore issues presented by the adolescent that do not necessarily fit neatly into diagnostic categories.

A clinician who can interweave the structured and unstructured portions of the middle phase of the interview process will be most successful at gaining all relevant information while not being repetitive. Within this context, the clinician who can make detailed observations while conversing with the adolescent, and who can intermix open questions with more direct and specific inquiries, will undoubtedly sustain greater concentration and attention by the adolescent to the task.

AA—C

Gathering Relevant Information

Blotcky (1984) has articulated seven important areas of assessment in interviewing an adolescent. These include "1) individual concerns, 2) family relationships, 3) peer relationships, 4) school performance, 5) extracurricular activities, 6) pathognomic indicators such as antisocial or bizarre behaviors, 7) ability to be self reflective" (Blotcky, 1984, p. 76). In assessing adolescents, it is important for the clinician to believe that no matter what level of pathology is presented, an understanding of their worldview is essential in formulating a diagnostic impression and in determining methods of intervention and remediation. Therefore, the following issues are also important to explore: (a) significant past life events; (b) previous attempts at coping with problems; (c) the adolescent's own assessment of current functioning; (d) the adolescent's assessment of her or his own personal health; and (e) outlook and goals for the future, including areas the adolescent desires to change and vocational aspirations. It is only with the cooperation of the adolescent, the decision to allow the clinician a window into his or her world, that the maximum benefit from a diagnostic interview can be realized.

Acute or Chronic Problems

Distinguishing between a chronic pattern of maladjustment and a recent inception of problem areas is crucial in determining an appropriate diagnostic classification. Specifically, it is beneficial to examine the adolescent's perceived level of distress and impairment and to assist the adolescent in making comparisons with past levels of adjustment (Blotcky, 1984). It is also helpful to ask the adolescent to directly enumerate three perceived strengths and three weaknesses and to determine if these have been long standing. Additionally, it is important to determine if there has been a recent precipitating event, such as a major loss (e.g., death of family member, suicide of friend), major trauma (e.g., divorce or parental separation, major health crisis necessitating a hospitalization) or radical change in the adolescent's daily life functioning (e.g., drug usage, relocation of family).

Bodily Concerns

Adolescence is a time when there is a great preocupation with one's own body. Part of this preoccupation is due to the rapid growth process that is experienced in adolescence, most notably including the onset of puberty. Gaining an understanding of the adolescent's view of his or her own body image and personal health can alert the clinician to consider possible diagnostic entities that may have been missed if inquiries of this nature had not been directly addressed. Questions regarding personal health include: (a) adolescent's own health assessment (e.g., does the individual possess any somatic complaints); (b) inquiries into personal habits (e.g., appetite, sleeping, hygiene); (c) inquiries into the experience of the onset of puberty (e.g., what was the adolescent female's reaction to beginning menstruation); and (d) questions about any health preoccupations (e.g., fears, recurring dreams).

Dealing with Previous Stressful Situations

Gaining information about prior significant life events and the adolescent's previous capacity to deal with the related stress allows for a longitudinal understanding of the adolescent's premorbid functioning. It can simultaneously provide a further delineation of the reasons the family currently feels at a level of crisis, and has been impelled to secure mental health services for their youngster. Inquiries into the adolescent's mechanisms for solving problems and coping with stress can also highlight the adolescent's strengths as well as indicate modes of maladaptive problem solving. If, for instance, the adolescent has had prior experience with mental health professionals, soliciting opinions about these services in terms of remediation of problem areas will also be beneficial in devising future plans for psychotherapeutic intervention.

Perceptions of the Family

Uncovering the adolescent's perceptions of his family is also an important component of making an overall assessment of the adolescent and his or her current situation. Issues such as how the youngster views his position in the family; who, in his or her opinion, constitutes the family entity; the manner in which daily family tasks are executed; perceived sources of power in the family, modes of communication and areas of conflict among family members; who in the family the adolescent is most worried about; recent family stressors; and previous family traumas all necessitate direct questioning by the clinician (Blotcky, 1984). The clinician must, however, be sensitive to the fact that some adolescents have difficulties in exploring these areas. At times they may feel like they are being disloyal to their parents if they comment negatively on family functioning. This is most salient in adolescents who reside within families where a member abuses alcohol or drugs, as these families are characterized by being extremely resistant to admitting difficulties, especially as it surrounds the substance abuse. For adolescents who demonstrate some hesitancy with regard to elaborating on family issues, the clinician should be supportive while at the same time encouraging the adolescent to discuss these concerns. It might be easier for the adolescent who is anxious about questions relating to family members to receive structured inquiries. For instance a request from the clinician such as "Tell me what it is like for you when your parents argue" may be less threatening than the question "Do your parents argue frequently?" as the former question does not require that the adolescent "snitch" on his or her parents. However, the adolescent may think that the clinician has prior information and that therefore the questions may reflect something very serious. Frequently, the adolescent's fears can be allayed by the clinician normalizing the situation by stating "these are questions I ask everyone I see in a first interview." Finally, the clinician must make it clear that the adolescent's views will not be shared with the parents, thus limiting the adolescent's concerns that there may be retaliation on the part of his or her parents for "spilling the beans."

Learning About Friendships

Gaining an understanding of the adolescent's quality of peer interactions is also important in terms of defining the appropriate diagnostic category. For example, the diagnostic category of Conduct Disorder, DSM-III-R (Spitzer & Williams, 1987) distinguishes between those class of youngsters displaying conduct disordered behaviors with a history of peer relationships (group type) with those who demonstrate a poverty of peer contacts (solitary type). It is important to ask the adolescent both the nature of current peer contacts and that of previous peer relationships. Adolescents who contend that they are able to make long-lasting peer relationships and have friends they feel close to and can confide in usually have a better prognosis than those individuals who have had difficulties sustaining friendships, are withdrawn from others and tend to operate on their own.

A clear understanding of the quality of the adolescent's peer relationships can best be obtained by asking specific questions. For instance, the clinician should not just accept at face value that the adolescent has a best friend, but should explore the issue further with such questions as: "How long have you been friends? ... Can you tell me what you like about this friend? ... Can you trust this friend? ... Can you tell this friend your problems?" By pursuing more detailed information, the clinician can distinguish between adolescents who can superficially present themselves in a favorable light (e.g., by answering that they do have a best friend), yet who, on closer inspection, do not manifest much intimacy with peers.

Sexual Involvement

Another important area of assessment is the quality and degree of sexual relationships (Blotcky, 1984). It is important in making assessments of an adolescent's interest in pursuing sexual relationships that the clinician be aware of the developmental stage of the adolescent. For example, continued sexual interactions for a 13-year-old may indicate maladaptive functioning, while this may not be so unusual for an adolescent of 18. As with other sensitive areas, the clinician who is straightforward and direct will be able to create an environment in which the adolescent will feel permission to discuss areas that are generally difficult to examine in an interpersonal context. Examples of direct questions include: "Do you have a boyfriend or girlfriend? ... Are you curious about sex? ... Have you had any sexual experiences such as kissing, fondling, intercourse? ... Have you had any homosexual experiences? ... Are you currently sexually active? ... Do you use any forms of birth control?" Again, assurances of confidentiality to the adolescent will be of assistance in gaining more accurate and detailed information.

School Problems

All adolescents spend a large portion of their time in school. In order to determine the adolescent's level of adjustment, an assessment must be made of his or her ability to both academically and socially function within the school setting (Blotcky, 1984). Important areas of identification with regard to academic functioning include: (a) level of current functioning in comparison to past performance (e.g., has there been a recent deterioration in academic performance); (b) ability to concentrate and attend to academic endeavors; (c) motivation to perform, and degree to which the adolescent's potential is reflected in actual achievement (e.g., is the adolescent an underachiever); and (d) vocational aspirations. The adolescent's social adjustment to school can be gauged by (a) ability to relate to fellow students and teachers; (b) overall conduct in the classroom; (c) the number of serious incidents in the school setting (either as instigator or victim); and (d) whether any truancy or school avoidance has been noted. Issues to take seriously include sustained school truancy, rapid deterioration in school performance, difficulties in concentration, alienation from teachers and students, aggressive behaviors toward students and school officials, and bizarre behaviors manifested in the school setting. Occasionally, information from the individual adolescent and family may not be comprehensive, and thus the clinician may decide to ask the adolescent and family for permission to contact the school directly. In these instances, releases of information must be signed by student and parents.

Level of Overall Activity

It is also important to examine the adolescent's activity level. For example, an understanding of the degree of activity the adolescent expends in extra-curricular endeavors may be helpful in diagnosing the presence of depression. If an adolescent presents with few friends, pervasive boredom and anhedonia, no specific interests or hobbies, and lack of plans for the future in terms of vocational placement, consideration of a depressive diagnosis might be seriously undertaken. It is important that the clinician inquire directly about the adolescent's recreational interests and not assume that "because the adolescent doesn't complain they must be satisfied." It is also essential that the clinician make an assessment of the nature of the adolescent's interests. For instance, a 14-year-old boy that still enjoys playing with toy trucks could be an indicator of potential maladjustment.

Elaborating on Specific Problem Areas

A line of questioning of pathological symptoms should also be undertaken. The adolescent should be asked to provide a detailed elaboration of referring problem areas. For instance, if the adolescent has engaged in delinquent activities, the clinician should ask for specifics such as: How often does she or he engage in such activities? Is she or he delinquent with peers or does she or he commit crimes alone? What is the nature of the crimes? What are her or his thoughts and feelings when engaging in such activities? The adolescent should also be directly questioned on other common symptom clusters. Specifically, for all adolescent interviews the clinician should inquire about (a) suicide ideation (present and past) and presence of a suicide plan; (b) homicidal ideation; (c) hallucination and delusions; (d) reality testing and confused thinking; (e) antisocial activities and acting-out behaviors; (f) preoccupations and persistent worries: (g) fears and phobias and (h) substance abuse. Many of these areas are covered in the Mental Status Exam, and the skilled clinician can usually interweave the formalized aspects of the Mental Status Exam (Siassi, 1984) while questioning about these symptom clusters.

Assessing Degree of Insight

Finally, it is important to gain an understanding of the adolescent's level of insight into problem areas and motivation to change. It is essential to assess the adolescent's ability to be self-reflective and to tolerate constructive external feedback. For example, a highly defensive, negative, impulsive, and externalizing adolescent with little capacity for insight would probably not make significant gains in a therapy modality which incorporated an uncovering and analytical approach. The clinician may, throughout the interview, offer some interpretive comments or challenging remarks, as a method of more directly assessing the adolescent's ability to be self aware and critical.

THE FINAL PHASE

Ending the Interview

Once all relevant information has been collected, it is important for the clinician to finalize the interview process with the adolescent. It is beneficial in ending the interview for the adolescent to be given the opportunity to ask any questions that may have been stimulated by the interview process. Some common adolescent inquiries include: (a) what the interviewer is going to do with the information, (b) how much of the information will be shared with the parents or guardians, and (c) what will be the next step after the completion of the interview. Some adolescents are also quite anxious about their performance in the interview and will ask for an assessment of their functioning. Occasionally the adolescent will also ask some personal questions about the interviewer. It is important that all questions be responded to in a serious and honest manner. Personal questions about the evaluator should be answered at the discretion of the clinician with consideration for the possible underlying motives of the adolescent. For example an adolescent asking if you have experience with other adolescents or have children of your own may be really wondering about your capacity to understand young people. As a final assessment tool, it is often helpful to get the adolescent's opinion of what would be a cogent plan for intervention. Such questions as "If you were in my position what would you recommend to help you and your family?" or "What kinds of things do you think would help you?" or "Let's say we are meeting a year from now, can you explain to me how you and your family solved the problems you are presently having?" These questions are based on the premise that the adolescent has within him or herself the ability to acknowledge appropriate mechanisms for making changes. The degree to which a clinician believes in this reasoning will vary; however, without the cooperation of the adolescent and his or her family, little progress can be made toward a more satisfactory level of adjustment. Thus, soliciting the clients' own ideas for treatment and intervention is an important component in the overall assessment process and in developing appropriate strategies for remediation.

Often, the clinician needs some time to reflect and synthesize the information before devising a treatment plan. It is important, however, to at least structure the next step in the process for the adolescent. For instance, the following can be explained to the adolescent at the end of the interview: "Well you have told me a lot today and you know that last week I met with you and your parents, and your parents alone. I have a lot of information from your family and I am going to go over that information. In a week I will have another appointment to go over with you and your family my recommendations for where to go from here. Do you have any further questions before we end?" It is important to note that the end of the interview is often a time of heightened anxiety for the adolescent and family, as they are often unsure of the next step in the process. Therefore it is incumbent on the clinician to offer as much clarification as possible.

Concluding Comments

The information obtained through the individual interview is very useful for specifically designing assessment batteries in order to further identify problem areas and delineate strategies for intervention. Individual interviews of adolescents also assist the clinician in developing probable hypotheses concerning the adolescent's family functioning, which can allow the clinician to develop more specific questions for interviewing the adolescent's family. Additionally, as initial interviews are usually the portal of entry for adolescents seeking psychotherapy, a well-conducted interview can precipitate a smooth transition into a more ongoing therapeutic experience. Thus, being skilled in the processes of interviewing adolescents is essential — as a tool for the clinician interested in designing effective prescriptive strategies for adolescent emotional disturbance, and as a way to increase the potential that the adolescent will be motivated to follow through on the devised treatment plan.

Chapter 3

Mental Status Exam

The Mental Status Exam is a more formalized interview procedure with the purpose of making a current assessment of the individual's mental functioning (Rosenthal and Akiskal, 1985). The categories of the Mental Status Exam were devised to structure the clinician's observations and inquiries in order to facilitate determination of an appropriate diagnostic formulation. While there are many variations of Mental Status Examinations, for the most part clinicians agree on the general categories inherent in this assessment procedure. Both Rosenthal and Akiskal (1985) and Siassi (1984) offer detailed and comprehensive outlines of Mental Status Examinations. This present discussion will be a compilation of the outlines proposed by these clinicians, with special attention to adolescent populations. The following categories of the Mental Status Exam will be detailed: (a) Appearance and Behavior, (b) Attitude Toward Interviewer, (c) Affect and Mood, (d) Speech and Thought, (e) Perception, (f) Orientation, (g) Attention, Concentration, and Memory, (h) Intelligence, and (i) Reliability, Judgment, and Insight.

Beginning clinicians often initially feel awkward in conducting a Mental Status Examination. Some common concerns involve being hesitant to ask the adolescent seemingly stilted questions such as orientation to person, place, and time. However, without being direct, subtle difficulties and symptoms may evade the clinician, leading to potential mistakes in diagnoses. For the most part, if the clinician is uneasy in conducting the examination, this increases the likelihood that the adolescent will not take the questioning seriously. It is best, therefore, to be well versed in the categories of the Mental Status Exam and comfortable in utilizing this assessment procedure before attempting to use a Mental Status Exam with an adolescent population. Additionally, offering the adolescent a cursory explanation of the exam may be of assistance in decreasing any potential anxiety generated by the structured questions. For example, the clinician could state "I am going to ask you some specific questions about your thoughts and feelings. I ask these questions of all people I interview. Some of these questions will remind you of tasks you are asked to complete in school." It is important to note that not all adolescents will need this explanation; in some cases it can make the adolescent more anxious if, for example school performance is an issue. The clinician must use his or her judgment in giving any prior explanation of the Mental Status Exam. As stated earlier, skilled clinicians can interweave the structure of the Mental Status Exam into the overall interview. While this is advantageous, the clinician should be careful when not proceeding in a systematic fashion that no categories of the exam are omitted.

CATEGORIES OF THE EXAM

Appearance and Behavior

The first category of the Mental Status Exam is Appearance and Behavior. As stated earlier, observation of the adolescent should begin at the inception of the interview. The nature of these observations should include assessments of: (a) general physical appearance and relation to actual chronological age, (b) grooming and dress, (c) mannerisms, (d) posturing, and (e) facial expressions (Rosenthal & Akiskal, 1985; Siassi, 1984). Any unusual markings, either physical or under the adolescent's volition (e.g., any tattoos, coordination of dress), should be noted. The adolescent's behavior should also be observed, such as activity level (e.g., agitated, restless, calm, psychomotor retardation). Additionally, an assessment of the adolescent's level of alertness should be made (e.g., Does the adolescent appear tired, intoxicated, hypervigilant?). In general, any unusual motor behavior should be recorded (e.g., persistent moving around in his or her seat, tearfulness, facial tics). While observation of appearance and behavior cannot lead directly to a comprehensive formulation, these assessments, made early in the interview process, can assist the clinician in formulating a variety of possible hypotheses regarding diagnosis.

Attitude Toward the Examiner

Throughout the interview, the quality of the adolescent's ability to engage with the clinician should be examined. Assessments should be made as to whether the adolescent presents as hostile, cooperative, friendly, suspicious, provocative, shy and withdrawn, or disinterested (Siassi, 1984). Attention should be paid as to whether the manner of relating to the clinician changes over the course of the interview. For example, is an adolescent who initially presents as guarded able to become more cooperative and revealing after she or he is familiarized with the interview process? The degree to which an individual rigidly holds on to a specific maladjusted or negative mode of interaction may also give further indication of the probable depth and chronicity of the pathology.

Affect and Mood

Many diagnostic entities require an assessment of affect and mood. Examination of affect requires the clinician's observation of the demonstrated "emotional tone" of the adolescent (Rosenthal & Akiskal, 1985, p. 30). Areas of consideration with regard to affect involve: (a) degree of affective liability, (b) degree of congruence between demonstrated affect and content of verbalizations, (c) degree of euphoria, irritability, hostility, anxiety, or depression presented, and (d) amount of blunted or "flat" emotional expression (Rosenthal & Akiskal, 1985). Mood, on the other hand, encompasses the adolescent's self report of predominant feeling state(s). The adolescent should be questioned as to the presence of such feelings as depression, euphoria, anxiety, agitation, anhedonia, anger, and hostility. Additionally, inquiries should be made as to the duration and intensity of these emotional states (Siassi, 1984). It would also be helpful if the adolescent is asked who else in the family displays similar moods and feelings, as some diagnostic categories seem to be prevalent through generations.

Speech and Thought

Speech and Thought encompass a broad area of examination. Observations of speech should include both manner of communicating and content of communications. Abnormalities of volume (e.g., loud, soft), speed (e.g., slow, rapid), force (e.g., pressured), content (e.g., inappropriate use of words, nonsensical words, circumstantiality) need to be recorded (Rosenthal & Akiskal, 1985). Frequently unusual speech patterns can alert the clinician to the possibility that the adolescent may manifest more severe pathology along the schizophrenic spectrum.

In making assessments of thought, the clinician needs to distinguish between thought processes (how the person thinks) from thought content (what the person thinks about). Rosenthal and Akiskal (1985) have delineated eleven general categories of abnormal thought processes with which the clinician should be familiar. They include: (a) circumstantiality, (b) tangentiality, (c) pressure of speech, (d) looseness of associations, (e) perseveration (continued verbalization of same thoughts), (f) echolalia (persistent repeating of a word or group of words), (g) confabulation (fabricating information), (h) thought blocking, (i) retardation or inhibition of thought processes, (j) mutism and (k) stupor (suspension of almost all motor activity), (l) aphonia and dysphonia (loss of voice not due to physical illness) (Rosenthal and Akiskal, 1985, pp. 32–34). Additional areas of concern entail racing thoughts, flight of ideas, and confused thinking; these are most notable in bipolar disturbance. Once again, many of these symptom clusters are most prevalent in more severe pathological conditions.

Assessing the nature of thought content is a very essential component of the Mental Status Exam. This encompasses inquiries concerning suicidal ideation and previous gestures, homicidal ideation, depression, feelings of inadequacy, delusions, obsessions and compulsions, preoccupations, phobias, paranoid ideation, grandiose reasoning, ideas of reference, and somatizations. Adolescents should be asked directly about these areas. Detailed information should be gathered as to the presence of any previous or current suicidal ideation, including the degree of intent to harm oneself, articulation of a plan, and seriousness of previous gestures. The clinician should be alert to the intensity and duration of any unusual and bizarre thought content. Assessments should be made as to whether the information presented by the adolescent requires immediate intervention in order to assure the individual safety of the adolescent and others.

Perception

Inquiries also need to be made concerning the presence of any disturbances of perception (Rosenthal & Akiskal, 1985). Hallucinations (e.g., visual, auditory, olfactory, tactile) are sensory experiences perceived by the individual but not actually present in the external environment. It is important that the clinician ascertain detailed information about the hallucinations, including most recent hallucination experienced, duration, and nature of hallucination. As with bizarre thought content, hallucinations usually indicate the presence of serious illness. However, often hallucinations are a symptom of an organic impairment, and the presence of a hallucination does not necessarily indicate severe psychopathology. It is essential that the clinician, once the adolescent has revealed that she or he experiences hallucinations, rule out the presence of any organic impairment by referring the adolescent for a complete physical exam. In working with adolescent populations, it is also important to make a distinction between disturbances of perception experienced under the influence of drugs and alcohol and those experienced when no mood-altering substances have been introduced into the adolescent's system. It is incumbent on the clinician to be very specific in the information gathered from the adolescent, so that no serious medical or drug dependency conditions are overlooked.

Orientation, Attention, Concentration and Memory

The components of the Mental Status Exam assessing orientation, attention, concentration and memory all function to make an appraisal of cognitive and sensorium functioning. Orientation is examined by asking the adolescent to answer questions regarding time (e.g., day, month, year), place (name of interview location, name of city, name of state), and person (what is interviewer's name) (Rosenthal & Akiskal, 1985). Difficulties in reporting this information to the clinician can again be a signal to alert the clinician that perhaps some seriously disturbed functioning is currently present in the adolescent. Additionally, it would also be important to make an assessment as to whether the adolescent is under the influence of some mood-altering agent which may temporarily cause disorientation.

A twofold approach should be undertaken in making an assessment of attention, concentration, and memory. The clinician should ask the adolescent to comment on those processes (e.g., Do you feel you have a good memory? ... Have you had any difficulties concentrating lately? ... Is it hard for you to attend to any one task for a sustained period of time?) as well as to ask the adolescent to demonstrate his or her abilities within the interview session. Attention can be examined mostly by observation (e.g., Does the adolescent seem easily distracted? Does he or she ask for questions to be repeated frequently?). Concentration can be examined by asking the adolescent to repeat a string of digits. Serial 7's, a task requiring the adolescent to continuously subtract 7 from a starting point of 100 until they reach the number 2 (younger adolescents can be given serial 3s starting at 30), can be employed to assess more sustained abilities of concentration. Finally, judgments of quality of memory need to encompass examinations of both recent and remote memory. Recent memory can involve asking the adolescent to remember the interviewer's name, what he or she had for breakfast, and what activity he or she engaged in after the previous school day. Conversely, remote memory encompasses previous life events, such as remembering a significant event in childhood or a significant event in history that occurred in their lifetime. It is important that the clinician be sensitive to the potential intrusion of anxiety, which may cause some impairment in the adolescent's functioning, on these components of the Mental Status Exam. The interviewer needs therefore to make a clinical judgment as to whether demonstrated deficits are a function of chronic impairments in attention, concentration, or memory, or a manifestation of difficulties dealing with situational anxiety. Occasionally it is helpful to repeat a task at a later point in the interview, thereby giving another referent with which to assess the adolescent's capacities.

Intelligence

Making a rough estimate of intellectual functioning is also another important area of the Mental Status Exam. Usually, the well-trained clinician has some sense of the adolescent's intellectual capabilities as a function of the interview process. However, occasionally guarded and highly defended adolescents are quite withholding, and can appear intellectually limited if assessment of cognitive functioning is entirely based on their verbal productions. If there is a question of intellectual abilities, the clinician can ask the adolescent some questions directed toward uncovering the adolescent's general fund of knowledge. Examples of some possible inquiries include: (a) Name four people who have been president of the United States, (b) Name three major U.S. cities, (c) How are an apple/orange/peach alike? and (d) How are a car/train/airplane alike? An evaluation of the adolescent's ability to abstract can be determined in part by soliciting their responses to proverbs. Some common proverbs appropriate to adolescent populations are: (a) can't judge a book by its cover, (b) a stitch in time saves nine, (c) a rolling stone gathers no moss, (d) people in glass houses shouldn't throw stones, (e) look before you leap, and (f) the grass is always greener on the other side of the fence. Assessments of intellectual level should also include inquiries into any recent deterioration in cognitive abilities, as this could alert the clinician to consideration of possible organic impairment.

Judgment, Insight, and Reliability

Finally, an evaluation of the degree of judgment, insight, and reliability of the adolescent needs to be undertaken (Rosenthal & Akiskal, 1985). The clinician must determine whether the adolescent's report can be viewed as reliable, or whether significant pathology (e.g., psychotic conditions) or malingering is contaminating the adolescent's assessment of his or her actual situation. Additionally, the clinician needs to determine the quality of the adolescent's insight into problem areas and motivation to change. The adolescent's ability to utilize insight and to make changes is, in part, a function of his/her judgment, which also must be examined. These areas are important factors in terms of determining the appropriate modality for intervention; consequently, they are the culminating components of the Mental Status Exam.

FINAL MENTAL STATUS REPORT

Once all the pertinent information is gathered, the clinician must organize the data and begin to formulate an appropriate diagnostic picture, while deciding appropriate strategies for intervention. An example of an abreviated report mostly organized from the Mental Status Exam portion of the interview is as follows:

Judy, a 15-year-old attractive adolescent female, is of tall and slender build. She was casually dressed; yet it seemed that she had not taken great interest in her appearance, as her hair was uncombed. Judy was brought to the clinic by her mother due to a recent history of pervasive complaints of fatigue, crying spells, and refusal to attend school. Upon introduction, Judy presented herself as shy, withdrawn, and reserved. She had difficulty making eye contact and often stared out the window even when she was answering interview questions. Periodically, Judy's attention seemed to wander, as she often asked for questions to be repeated. While Judy was generally compliant with interview procedures, she tended to respond in a short and concise manner. Frequently, further probing was necessary by the interviewer in order to ascertain the full meaning of her response. Judy spoke in a slow and hesitant manner. She often was tearful and sighed in-between verbalizations. Throughout the interview, Judy maintained a rather distant and withdrawn stance with regard to establishing a relationship with the evaluator, as she seemed generally preoccupied with her own internal thoughts.

Initially Judy was vague about both the duration and intensity of the presenting symptoms. While she maintained that she was unsure about any precipitating event, it seemed that there was a specific crisis that had ensued. Judy, however, was hesitant and fearful of revealing the specific situation. As it appeared to the evaluator that Judy displayed many of the symptoms consistent with adolescents who have been sexually abused, questions regarding any recent abuse were addressed. At first, Judy did admit to replaying an event over and over in her mind, but refused to detail the event. When questioned about her specific concerns, Judy was able to verbalize that she was worried about hurting her parents by them thinking that she was a "bad girl." With support, Judy was finally able to briefly describe being sexually molested by a male peer at school. Her initial ambiguity regarding recent events did not therefore appear a product of difficulties with memory but more a function of extreme fearfulness about revealing the trauma in the interview forum. With continued support, Judy was able to acknowledge a deterioration in her everyday functioning since the "incident", and the development of a tremendous amount of fearfulness with regard to retribution on the part of her perpetrator if she revealed this information. The limited information Judy provided did agree with her mother's temporal reports of her decrease in adjustment and overall functioning. Her mother had stipulated that Judy had been a "straight A" student who was interested in school up until a month ago, when she had begun to insist on staying home due to complaints of illness and had refrained from completing any schoolwork.

Throughout the interview, Judy's affect was anxious and depressed. Her verbalized mood was that of sadness and great concern about her future. Both her emotional expressions (e.g., tearfulness) and the content of her responses indicated a youngster who was quite overwhelmed by issues of sadness and anxiety. Judy admitted to both disturbances of sleep, always feeling fatigued but having difficulties falling asleep, and appetite, feeling a reduced need to eat. Judy also admitted to feelings of helplessness and hopelessness. While she affirmed that she felt so depressed that she had recently considered suicide, she was vague as to the manner in which she would consider doing herself harm. Judy maintained that she was preoccupied with concerns of being harmed and in being considered by others as a "bad girl;" however, Judy was hesitant to elaborate on the basis for these feelings. Judy denied any homicidal ideation and any disturbances of perception, including auditory or visual hallucinations. There was no evidence suggestive of circumstantiality, tangentiality, or looseness of associations in her thinking processes. Judy did display some paranoid ideation, feeling that she would be attacked again, but given the recent trauma she had incurred this seemed like a fairly normal response. Reality testing therefore appeared largely intact.

While it took Judy a considerable amount of time to answer questions regarding orientation to time/place/person, she was oriented X3. Judy had difficulties concentrating, and as already noted, she was somewhat distractible throughout the interview. She attempted serial 7's three times and on all trials was not successful. She also displayed difficulties in concentration when asked to repeat a string of digits. These difficulties seemed situationally based, as Judy until recently had an outstanding scholastic record. In direct questioning of fund of knowledge, Judy displayed above average intellectual capabilities which is consistent with her school history. She answered proverbs in an abstract yet personalized manner. Her response to the proverb "can't judge a book by its cover" entailed "a person who seems honorable on the surface, may actually hurt you" and seemed to further reveal her current sense of fearfulness and preoccupation with impending harm. Judy did seem to manifest some insight into her problem areas. While her judgment was somewhat impaired in terms of telling family members or other professionals of abuse, she basically had been a well adjusted youngster prior to this trauma. Additionally, there was no observable evidence to suggest that her recounting of events was anything but accurate and reliable.

In summary, Judy presents as a depressed and anxious youngster. The inception of her difficulties was clearly marked by an incident of sexual molestation by a school peer. She had been hesitant and fearful to share this incident with family members and school officials, as she was concerned about retribution by her assailant. Her clinical picture is consistent with a diagnosis of Post Traumatic Stress Disorder. The severity of her symptoms including pervasive anxiety, persistent sleep and appetite disturbance, and thoughts of self harm indicate that a short term hospitalization will be beneficial in assisting Judy in gaining a more satisfactory stabilization of her emotional reaction. Judy and her family are in agreement with the need for a short hospitalization, as they feel they need some assistance in dealing with the acute level of her distress. Both her level of insight, degree of perceived distress, and her ability to accurately reality test indicate that the prognosis is favorable.

The Mental Status Exam by itself usually is not adequate to fully determine the nature of the presenting problems and develop an appropriate intervention plan. However, Mental Status Exams do allow clinicians a more systematic and structured approach for exploring the cognitions and thought processes of adolescents. The Mental Status Exam is an important component of the process of conducting individual interviews of adolescents, as its aim is to begin to identify probable diagnostic impressions of the youngsters. Therefore, Mental Status Exams can provide pertinent information to clinicians prior to administering psychological test batteries, thus allowing clinicians to more specifically tailor individual psychological assessments.

Chapter 4

Conducting Family Interviews

ESTABLISHING RAPPORT

In assessing adolescents it is often important to gather information about the family. Adolescents are part of many systems (e.g., family, school, peers) and it is essential that their position in these contexts be reviewed. Parents and family members can be utilized to supply information that broadens the assessment to include the different systems in which the adolescent resides. Limiting the assessment process to an individual interview and administration of evaluation instruments, gives the clinician only a small sample of the adolescent's behavior. By adding a family interview, the clinician can compare the directly observed behavior to behavior within the adolescent's environment, thus contributing to a more integrated conceptualization of the adolescent's functioning.

As with conducting individual interviews with adolescents, it is important in meeting with the family to establish an atmosphere where family members can feel comfortable in sharing pertinent personal information. It is the responsibility of the clinician to structure the interview so that anxiety and fears of negative evaluation are minimized, and a sense of trust and safety maximized. In order to decrease some of the probable anxieties, resistances and misconceptions the family brings to the interview, it is best for the clinician to be initially more active in providing a structural framework.

The first step is to help the family feel comfortable in the interview room. This is a time for social amenities to be exchanged and for each family member to be introduced to the clinician. Often the best way to conceptualize this first stage is to imagine that the family just walked into your living room and you were beginning the process of getting to know them. You would probably make sure each person had a seat, find out everybody's name, and any nicknames people prefer; ask them about their trip over to your home, and finally share some information about yourself. In the interview situation, these same social gestures are also shared. To a family that is either anxious or embarassed about needing to be seen by a clinician, these subtle gestures can be quite powerful in reducing tension and elevating the family's status.

After introductions have been completed, it is beneficial to provide the family with a framework for the interview process. This usually encompasses describing to the family the probable length, the format, and some of the goals of the interview. Once this has been explained to the family, the clinician can begin. It is usually best, in interviewing families with adolescents as the identified client, to offer a brief but straightforward accounting of the information gained through the referral process. The following is an example of an introduction in the family interview.

> Dr. Lane: I'm glad everyone could make it today. Before we begin I wanted to tell you all what will happen here today. I've asked you to come to meet with me so I could get an understanding of what seems to be the problems you are experiencing. We probably will be meeting for about an hour and a half. During that time I would like to find out what each one of you thinks about how things are going in the family—both your likes and dislikes. As you know I was called by your parents to conduct an assessment of David. Before I begin with David, I wanted to get a sense of your whole family. Specifically, what is happening now in the family, how you developed as a family, what have been the major events in the life of the family, and how members see the family presently functioning. I want to make sure everyone has a chance to talk. Are there any questions before we begin? ... O.K. Let's begin. First it would be a good idea if I tell you what I know already so we can all start at the same place. The other day I was called by Mrs. M. because she was concerned about you, David. Her concerns centered on you having difficulties doing the chores she asked you to do around the home, and doing poorly in school including grades and behavior. She also expressed to me that it is difficult for your sisters and you to get along. I also know that you just moved to this area in September, that you Mr. M., work hard and frequently your job takes you out of town. Now I'm interested in how everyone else sees things.

After such an introduction, the "family representative" (usually the member who initially solicited services) often begins the interview, supplying further information (Stierlin et al., 1980). Then the clinician can begin to work his or her way around to each family member.

If the "family representative" does not initially volunteer, it is best to pick one of the parents and begin questioning them. It is usually not a good idea to turn to the identified client (referred adolescent), as the pressure they are already experiencing is enormous and the clinician, in the early stages of the interview, may want to indirectly demonstrate to the family that the identified client may only be a symptom of a breakdown of the family system. In shy and reserved families, it may be best for the clinician to choose a seemingly neutral family member to begin the interview.

Engaging Resistant Families

There are occasional families who, even with the clinician's initial structuring, are not forthcoming in the interview. It may be difficult for these families to involve themselves in an interview process if they rigidly define their youngster as the problem. They may remind the clinician that they have sought an *individual* evaluation of their adolescent and thus occasionally parents may react to the request for a family interview by simply questioning the utility of such a request to refusing to participate in this type of interview. Families who demonstrate these resistances are usually angry or very pathological families in which resentment, mistrust of outsiders, and poor intrafamilial communication are paramount. These families frequently have had prior experience (often negative) with mental health professionals and community agencies. They may even have been labeled by other clinicians as "treatment failures." Additionally, they may have been coerced into soliciting services either by the school system, which has threatened to expel their youngster, or perhaps through the court system, which has mandated an evaluation or therapy. Even though these families may not be as open to the interview process as families that come on their own volition, it is important that the clinician treat them with the same respect. They are usually quite sensitive to any negative feedback, and to the degree that they perceive that they are being negatively judged they will place further obstacles in the evaluation process. It is therefore essential that the clinician be especially conscious of creating an atmosphere of mutual respect and trust.

In working with these potentially resistant families in the interview situation, McGoldrick and Gerson (1985) have developed an important interviewing strategy. They maintain that in resistant or problematic families, "reframing or detoxifying family issues" may be of assistance in facilitating disclosures of family functioning (McGoldrick & Gerson, 1985, p. 133). In general this strategy involves normalizing the family's experience to decrease the need for the family to react in a defensive manner (McGoldrick & Gerson, 1985). For example in a family which is experiencing difficulty starting the interview, the clinician could offer the following statement, "You know, raising adolescents is the hardest job a parent has to face in the life cycle of the family. How has it been for you?" In this example, the clinician normalizes the parents' struggles while at the same time questioning them on their feelings.

For families that have been coerced into an assessment or treatment, the clinician could reframe the situation by stating, "I know the court has asked you to come see me today, but you obviously are here because you care about your child. I'm interested in the ideas you have on how to help your child get over this difficult period." The clinician, in this example, concentrates on the positive steps the family has taken (i.e., complying with the court order), thus elevating the family's status. Involving oneself in the power struggle between the court and the family will only increase the family's defensiveness. A family that senses that the clinician is interested in the positive aspects of its functioning will have a harder time remaining in a resistant and guarded position. It is only by feeling valued and empowered that defensive families can begin to trust the interviewer, thus allowing for a more spontaneous sharing of important family patterns and events.

OBTAINING RELEVANT INFORMATION

Once the introductions have been completed and a rapport established with family members, the focus of the interview shifts to gathering more specific information in order to develop an understanding of the family and social environment in which the adolescent resides. In the middle phase of the interview, the clinician is obtaining information on the family's functioning, both through individual members' verbalizations and through observation of direct family interactions during the actual interview. During this phase the clinician must strike a balance between structuring the interview questions such that certain information can be elicited and allowing the family some freedom in "telling their story," so that more spontaneous family patterns of communication and interaction can be observed.

Clarifying the Presenting Complaints

It is usually most helpful to begin this phase by asking for an elaboration of the presenting complaints. Detailed information should be collected as to the precipitants, nature, and duration of the stated problem areas. Each family member should be questioned concerning their understanding of the presented complaints. The family should be probed as to the reason why the problem has currently resulted in the need for an outside evaluation and assistance. In addition, a review of previous attempts by the family to cope with the problem (e.g., past evaluations, previous contact with mental health agencies, with extended family, clergy, and/or hospitalizations) should be investigated. McGoldrick and Gerson (1985) have developed useful questions regarding the presenting complaints, in order to assess the current nature of the problem within the context of the family. They include: a) which family members know about the problem? b) how does each view it, and how has each of them responded? c) has anyone in the family had similar problems? and d) what solutions were tried and by whom? (p. 31). Chloe

Madanes (1986) maintains that asking about what would transpire if the problem worsened or was eradicated can also yield important information about both the role of the adolescents symptom as well as the role the symptomatic member plays for the family. Her line of questioning includes gaining information from the family concerning: a) who would first notice if the problem went away, who would notice last; b) who would be upset if the problem was solved, what the consequences would be if it got solved; c) who would be upset if the problem worsened; d) if there is a part of the problem that anyone would want to keep; e) who is most and who is least concerned about the problem, and why; and f) what instead of problem behavior would the family consider normal and age appropriate (Madanes, 1986). It is also often helpful to ask family members what would occupy their time or consititue their pressing worries if the problem was solved. The clinician who asks both directly and indirectly about the problem from each family member's perspective will gain a more comprehensive understanding of the function of the symptom the adolescent has adopted. In other words, the role of the symptom within the context of the family will become clearer.

Obtaining a Family History

Once the family's current situation is clarified, it is important for the clinician to gain a sense of the family's history and the nature of the relationships between family members both actual and emotional. McGoldrick and Gerson (1985) maintain that construction of the family genogram can be a useful tool in gathering and understanding the structure and history of the family. They have articulated interpretive categories in the genogram interview which assesses present and past family organization and dynamics. Some of these categories encompass:

I.   *Family Structure* — the actual construction of the family genogram (or family tree) revealing information on family constellation including recording biological, marital and adopted relationships, sibling position, record of births, deaths and divorces.

II. *Life Cycle Fit* — including gathering information on how the family has negotiated through the stages of family life cycle (e.g., courtship, marriage, birth of children) and dealt with individual developmental stages of family members (e.g., infancy, latency, adolescence).

III. *Pattern Repetition Across Generation* — assessment of similarities within family members across generations (e.g., incidences of mental and medical illnesses in the family, prevalence of divorce, patterns in the quality of relationships between same sex and opposite sex family members).

IV. *Life Events and Family Functioning* — includes obtaining information on the impact of major life events (e.g., births, deaths, divorces, relocation, economic hardships) and the anniversaries of those events on the life of the family.

These four categories involve uncovering a sense of the family's history as well as soliciting the family's conceptualization of the impact of this history on their present functioning. It is exactly this context which is effected by and effects the adolescent.

Assessing Family Relationships

Direct questioning of present familial relationships is essential in terms of developing a comprehensive assessment of the adolescent's social environment. McGoldrick & Gerson (1985) label this process as determining familial "relational patterns and triangles" (p. 159). Madanes (1986) advocates asking each family member questions such as: a) who gets along better with whom? b) who is closer to whom? c) who is further apart? d) who tells whom what to do? e) who tries to please whom? f) what do they like about each other? g) how do they help each other? h) what do they worry about each other? and i) who does each resemble? Madanes (1986) also advocates asking about contact with extended family, both the quality and quantity of such contacts. This is usually the place in the interview where questions regarding the marital relationship (e.g., level of marital discord, manner in which marital unit has negotiated problem areas) and the relationship the parents have individually with their children (e.g., is one parent overidentified with a particular child) are addressed (McGoldrick & Gerson, 1985). It is important to note that this portion of the family interview may be the most uncomfortable for the family, as it asks members to comment on their relationships with other members in the room. Discretion should be used by the clinician as to what constitutes an appropriate level of questioning, given the family structure. For example, more sensitive marital issues would be best discussed between marital couple and clinician rather than in the context of the whole family. Consequently, it may be advisable to conduct a part of the interview alone with the parents. As adolescents may be sensitive to the clinician meeting alone with their parents, the clinician can directly articulate that the meeting will encompass those issues that pertain only to the adults in the family.

Assessment of family relationships should also be based on the clinician's own observations of the family's interactional patterns during the actual interview. The family interview presents a forum for direct observations of family communication and interactional patterns. It is within that context that the clinician can begin to compare the family's verbalizations concerning their relationships with the actual interactional patterns which are displayed throughout the interview process. Loarder, Burck, Kinston and Bentovim (1982) have developed a method for organizing the observations of family interactions during an interview. Those categories which are pertinent to the evaluation of family relationships include:

I. *Atmosphere* — assessment based on the overall relationship between the family and clinician and between individual family members which includes the clinician's subjective reaction to the family, predominant affective mood the family projects (e.g., do family members appear guarded, angry or sad) and the emotional tone (e.g., do they feel comfortable or ill at ease with one another).

II. *Communication* — assessment of patterns of communication which involves observation of verbal and nonverbal interchanges between family members (e.g., degree of congruence between verbal and nonverbal cues), quality and quantity of messages given and manner in which interchanges are initiated and transmitted.

III. *Affective States* — assessment of the degree to which individual family members express their emotional reactions, are responded to, and can communicate about their feelings.

IV. *Boundaries* — assessment of the appropriateness of intergenerational boundaries (e.g., are parents in charge or have they relinquished power to their children), quality of relationships between family members (emeshed vs. disengaged), and boundaries between family and outside world.

V. *Alliances* — assessment of the quality of the relationships between family members (e.g., marital relationship, parent-child relationships and sibling relationships).

By contrasting the family's verbalizations of their functioning with direct observations, the clinician can develop a broader context from which to evaluate both the adolescent's role in the family as well as the family's impact on the adolescent.

Assessing Current Family Functioning

Finally, the family interview should center on the family's current functioning. McGoldrick and Gerson (1985) conceptualize this as determining the family's balance and imbalance. This entails uncovering the presence or absence of family resources (e.g., are monetary resources severely limited), day-to-day functioning (e.g., does the family sit down to meals together) and organization (e.g., how is discipline of the children handled). It also involves making assessments of the individual family members' functioning. For example, it is important to determine the presence of serious medical or mental illness in family members, the pattern of work history among the parents and patterns of school history with the children, family's use or abuse of drugs and alcohol, and any experiences of difficulties with the law

(McGoldrick & Gerson, 1985). A history of these problem areas must include the duration, nature, and previous attempts at solving these difficulties. It is important to ask about these areas specifically, as they significantly impact on family functioning but may not be initially presented to the clinician by the family as problem areas. For example, an adolescent may be engaging in delinquent behavior which has motivated the family to seek an evaluation of their child, however, only when the family is directly asked is the mother's alcoholism disclosed.

The quality of family functioning can also be assessed through direct observation of family members during the interview process. Loader et al., (1982) have developed two categories pertinent to this issue: parental function and family operations. They refer to the day-to-day processes of the family, exemplified in the interview hour by witnessing such behaviors as: how the parents obtain the children's cooperation with the evaluation process; how the parents discipline the children if they misbehave during the interview; how the family resolves conflict and deals with anger (Loader et al., 1982). With respect to parental function, the clinician needs to determine the degree to which the "executive branch" of the family is able to accomplish the task of parenting. Assessments need to be made regarding the degree to which the couple supports, agrees with, and cooperates with each other on parenting practices (Loader et al., 1982). This category also represents the degree to which the parents are effective at caring for their children. Inadequacies in setting appropriate parental rules and in following through on realistic consequences when regulations are violated often characterize families with severely acting out adolescents. Similarly, family operations (the degree to which the family can engage in adequate problem solving, can mediate conflict between members, can adjust to developmental life cycle tasks, and can make decisions) also involves parental direction in order for ongoing, successful outcome in family functioning (Loader et al., 1982). In other words if conflict is poorly dealt with on the parental level, there will be a marked inadequacy in overall family operations.

The family's relationship to the larger external environment is another essential area for the clinician to explore, as it reveals an important aspect of the family's overall functioning (Loader et al., 1982). Both the quality and quantity of the family's external supports need to be evaluated. This involves obtaining information concerning the nature of the family's involvement with relatives, friends, and community organizations (e.g., church or syna-gogue, support groups, recreational facilities). Families that are emotionally isolated from relatives and the community tend to have greater difficulty tolerating stress. Concomitantly, parents who feel isolated and alone tend to have smaller emotional reserves with which to offer their children support and guidance during times of stress. It is important to thoroughly evaluate the external environmental supports the family has established, as they may serve as valuable resources for assisting the adolescent and family in restabilizing.

Evaluating environmental resources also involves an analysis of the family's previous relationship(s) with mental health professionals. The clinician should question the family as to under what conditions did the family feel prompted to solicit services, who presented at that time as the identified patient, and what was the quality and duration of the services. It is important for the clinician to gain an understanding of how mental health professionals were utilized within the context of the family (e.g., is this a family which contacts professionals at the slightest provocation, are they a "revolving door" family who seek services in crisis but then do not follow through to resolve problem areas) and to assess the degree of motivation currently presented by the family to eradicate the stress and tension exhibited by the adolescent.

If no previous treatment has been solicited, observations should be made concerning the manner in which the family has interacted with the clinician during the actual interview as this offers a sample of the probable relationship the family would initiate in an ongoing therapeutic encounter (Loader et al., 1982). This is important information as the clinician at the end of the family interview and assessment process of the adolescent will be in a position of making recommendations. For example a family which presents as being resistant and hostile may need some additional assistance in accepting a recommendation for therapy. If an assessment can be made concerning the family's probable toleration for outside assistance during the initial evaluation, strategies can be implemented which are directed toward decreasing the hesitancy of the family before the family. This increases the potential that the family will cooperate in recommendations for their involvement in any proposed treatment strategies following completion of the overall assessment of the adolescent.

TERMINATING THE INTERVIEW

Initiating, conducting, and finally terminating a family interview involves many complex processes. A successful termination of a family interview is predicated on the fact that the clinician has been able to observe, listen to, and interact with the family. The purpose of the family interview, within the context of an evaluation of an adolescent, is to uncover the history, structure, organization and current functioning of the youngster's family. By gathering this information in conjunction with an individual interview and formalized testing procedures, the clinician will be able to develop specific recommendations which take into consideration the many systems of which the adolescent is a part.

In closing the family interview, it is again important for the clinician to take a leadership role. When a family assessment is part of an evaluation of an adolescent, recommendations will obviously be delivered to the parents after completion of the entire assessment process. Therefore it is best to end the interview by briefly summarizing information obtained and in reviewing with the family the schedule for future evaluation sessions of the adolescent and the interpretive interview in which the evaluation will be shared with the parents. While presenting recommendations to the family is the focus of Chapter 9, it is important to note that the ability of the clinician to present a well formulated and acceptable treatment plan is dependent on information gathered through the formalized evaluation process as well as obtained through the family interview. The clinician who makes genuine contact with each family member and who is respectful to the family increases the likelihood that presented recommendations will be accepted and followed through by the family. It is therefore most helpful for the clinician to view the assessment interview with the family as a forum both for gathering information and for introducing the family into the process of family therapy. By making family members more familiar with this process and stimulating more open disclosures, the assessment interview can be a quite powerful modality in beginning the journey toward more positive adjustment in the adolescent through more harmonious family functioning.

Chapter 5

Principles of
Psychological Testing

TESTING WITHIN THE
ASSESSMENT PROCESS

Within the process of assessing adolescents, the need arises to objectively understand their intellectual and emotional strengths and weaknesses, as well as to supply information on how these abilities and deficits may impact on their daily functioning. In response to this need, an extensive array of standardized techniques has evolved to aid the examiner in: measuring intelligence (e.g., the Wechsler Intelligence Scale for Children-Revised [Wechsler, 1974]); screening for perceptual–motor dysfunction (e.g., the Bender Visual-Motor Gestalt Test [Bender, 1938]); gauging educational level (e.g., the Wide Range Achievement Test Revised [Jastak & Wilkinson, 1984]); evaluating severe emotional pathology (e.g., the Rorschach Inkblots [Rorschach, 1942]) and delineating personality descriptions (e.g., the Minnesota Multiphasic Personality Inventory [MMPI] [Hathaway & McKinley, 1967]). The major purpose of all these devices (i.e., psychological tests) is to elaborate upon the causes and degree of the disturbance(s) in question, in order to better formulate desirable treatment plans.

The introduction of psychological testing into the assessment process provides objective information on the skills and performances of adolescents. Testing, narrowly defined, considers only the technical aspects of administration. From a broader perspective, testing can be viewed as a more complex interaction of interpreting and integrating the results of all segments of the formal test battery (Cronbach, 1970).

The primary value of psychological tests lie in their objectivity, where they attempt to reduce the possible distortions that frequently occur in clinical judgments through omissions and subjective biases (Berger, 1976). However, no test is ever totally free of error. A certain amount of inaccuracy will always occur when attempting to measure an individual's abilities or personality traits (Stanley, 1971). These errors can occur either systematically or at random. Some tests have a tendency to produce systematically high or low scores, which then misrepresent the abilities or characteristics of the adolescent being tested. Other tests may be inconsistent in that the resulting scores may differ on a daily basis or may change with a different examiner.

When important decisions are being considered based on the results of unreliable test instruments, those decisions have to be questioned. In addition, the examiner must have a rationale in the selection of a particular test in order to guarantee that the test is used appropriately. Furthermore, if the examiner does not understand the assumptions upon which a specific test is based, the results can be overgeneralized (e.g., using the Peabody Picture Vocabulary Test-Revised [Dunn, 1981] as a measure of generalized intelligence).

NORMATIVE DATA

Psychological tests have meaning only when compared with certain explicit criteria (Anastasi, 1982). The adolescent can either be judged by his or her own individual performance on a specific test or by comparing the obtained scores against a group standard of similar youths in parallel environments (i.e., a reference group). A common example of using an adolescent's own test results as the criterion is seen when trying to ascertain treatment effectiveness: for instance, one may solicit information from parents and teachers using a behavior checklist, before and after the youth has been placed on medication. Most psychological instruments have attempted to include comparisons of peers of the same age or school level. These standardization samples attempt to be representative as to racial, ethnic, and socieconomic backgrounds, as well as geographic locations. However, the idea of gathering representative samples whose characteristics will be suitable to a cross-section of students is extremely difficult, since any limited sample cannot hope to represent the entire range of youth or even all tenth graders.

THE DEVELOPMENT OF SCALES

The most common-sense approach to test construction is simple face validity (Golden, Sawicki, & Franzen, 1984). The most basic case is the scale that attempts to focus on a single dimension. The items that are chosen for this scale are assumed to measure this one dimension, and these items typically differ only in degree of difficulty. In some instances, this range of difficulty implies that errors made during the beginning of the scale will persist on the remaining items. An example is the Benton Visual Retention

Test. While all of its designs are assumed to represent visual–motor functioning, they appear to be arranged by level of difficulty. Another example would be a depression scale where the items seem to appear relevant to the general symptoms of depression (e.g., feeling sad or blue; early awakening).

RELIABILITY AND VALIDITY

Whatever test is being used, it must meet two essential statistical criteria: reliability and validity. A test only becomes reliable when scores are produced consistently, or when a similar score is obtained on multiple testings of the same individual. Tests of intelligence, for example, would not be reliable if the IQ fluctuated more than 20 or 30 points on a repeat testing over a short period of time. Correlation coefficients based on test–retest administrations, split-half methods, and alternate forms versions of a particular test provide important information for the examining psychologist to evaluate before choosing a test to administer. A generally accepted minimum level of reliability for psychological tests is estimated at approximately + .80 or better.

The concept of validity in test construction is generally conceived as indicating that the test is actually measuring what it purports to measure. In practice, however, most questions of validity are based on whether a particular test is capable of predicting performance in a criterion situation. For example, since the idea of intelligence is controversial, with varying definitions and assumptions, tests of intelligence are typically validated against school performance.

Psychological tests are usually validated in four different ways to specify that a relationship does exist between the test performance and a criterion measure. These include predictive, concurrent, content, and construct validity. Predictive validity is a way of describing the degree to which a test anticipates some future behavioral event, such as the aforementioned relationship between IQ and school achievement. Oftentimes new tests are validated by establishing correlations between their own results with scores from tests of proven validity. Such is the case when scores from new intelligence tests are correlated with scores from the WISC-R or Stanford-Binet. This technique offers confirmation for the concurrent validity of the test. Content validity is an evaluative technique that attempts to discover whether a particular test is representative in its inclusion of a specific content area. Comprehensive achievement tests in a single subject are good illustrations of the uses of this type of concept. By comparison, personality terms such as extroversion and anxiety, which constitute tests of individual differences, are theoretical constructs. The extent that a test conforms to the theories of that construct is its construct validity.

SELECTING A TEST BATTERY

The decision as to which tests to administer varies according to referral questions, the referral source and agency involved, time constraints, and other situational factors. A battery of tests is usually selected in order to permit the examiner the opportunity to observe performances in a wide area of test-taking situations and allow the adolescent the chance to express his or her abilities and levels of functioning. Responses from an individual test cannot be expected to answer all the relevant questions that have been posed by the clinicians attempting to formulate a diagnosis and treatment strategy. Additionally, no single instrument can measure all abilities of an individual, some of which may be concealed by the presenting problems.

Most psychologists tend to re-use the same set of tests with which they have been trained and have become comfortable with over time. Through repeated usage, these tests provide the psychologist with a personal baseline for comparing normal versus abnormal functioning. Although a particular set of tests may be useful in delineating problem areas in most clinical cases, there are many instances in which a variety of other specialized tests are needed for handicapping conditions. The examiner needs to be aware of these alternative tests in addition to being kept informed of new tests and revised normative data on existing tests. By keeping abreast of developments in the field of psychometrics, examiners can enhance their usefulness to the adolescent and his or her family.

Besides the specific tests already discussed, which measure intelligence, educational achievement, brain impairment, personality disorder, and severe emotional disturbance, the realization of the complexity between brain and behavior has initiated a movement in psychology toward the use of extended neuropsychological batteries (e.g., the Halstead-Reitan). These groups of individual tests attempt to assess specific deficits in abilities relating to motor coordination, memory, attention, flexibility in thinking, and other problems in information processing. Since the problems of adolescents tend to be multifaceted, neuropsychological testing can be a major influence in helping a youth with brain damage or some aspect of learning dysfunction and his or her family comprehend the problem(s) in a more objective manner. Additionally, by providing more specific information, teachers can focus on an adolescent's areas of strength in establishing educational and behavioral objectives.

CONCLUSION

In its purest sense, the development of psychological tests entails a series of interrelated steps ranging from theoretical assumptions, item development and choice, and statistical methodology, to normative investigations. This process evolves beyond the initial scale construction to continual refinements in order to enhance the general usability of the device. This constant upgrading is required since no test is ideal, and each setting, individual need, and group is different (Golden, Sawicki, & Franzen, 1984). The ideal in test development includes research that guarantees that a particular test is appropriate to a specific sample and clinical issues, in addition to empirical feedback that helps ensure maximum clinical utility.

Chapter 6

Intellectual and Educational Assessment

Referrals for the psychological evaluation of adolescents frequently include questions that can only be answered by assessment of both intellectual and academic functioning. Given the central place of school performance in an adolescent's life, questions concerning behavioral and emotional problems, as well as academic underachievement, require information about the adolescent's cognitive abilities and actual levels of school achievement. The examiner, therefore, needs to be familiar with the technical aspects of both types of assessments and with the broader issues surrounding their use.

INTELLIGENCE TESTS AND THE NATURE OF INTELLIGENCE

Part of the continuing controversy over the use of intelligence tests stems from the lack of an agreed-upon definition of the concept of intelligence. Attempts have been made to define intelligence in terms of a set of highly valued cognitive abilities; however, different experts stress different sets of abilities, and the role of noncognitive variables has not been established. Although it is beyond the scope of this book to explore these various definitions of intelligence, the views of Wechsler (1958) provide a frame of reference for the following discussion of the intellectual assessment process.

Wechsler defines intelligence as the overall or global capacity of an individual to "comprehend the world and deal effectively with its challenges". Being a global capacity, intelligence is seen as a multidetermined and multifaceted function of the personality as a whole, rather than any particular set of intellectual abilities. Nonintellective traits such as persistence, anxiety, or goal awareness are factors of intelligence, since they act to enhance or inhibit the expression of other abilities. Wechsler (1974) makes the further point that intelligence is not an ability at all but rather is something inferred from the way these abilities are manifested under different circumstances and conditions. Since intelligence can be manifested in many ways, an adequate measure of it should utilize many different tests.

IQ scores are not direct measures of innate intelligence. Rather, they are imperfect measures of a limited sample of an individual's developed abilities at a particular point in time. They are not immutable, but rather subject to change and sensitive to what a person has been exposed to through interaction with his or her culture. IQ scores are, therefore, estimates of an individual's current level of functioning on the types of tasks included in the assessment. Most commonly used intelligence tests measure, primarily, verbal abilities, and to a lesser extent perceptual organizational skills and the ability to manipulate numerical and other symbols. These tests do not adequately measure other abilities considered "intelligent" — for example, social awareness, musical talent, mechanical aptitude, and artistic abilities.

These limitations should be kept in mind when discussing the results of an intellectual assessment. Language that would encourage the reification of test scores should be avoided. Instead of saying "she has an IQ of 95" it is more exact to say "she obtained a score of 95 on this test" or, perhaps better yet, "she obtained a score in the average range on this test". Since the scores are measures of current functioning, retesting is important if placement decisions are influenced by IQ scores or if significant changes in an individual's functioning are anticipated. Because the scores are sensitive to cultural experiences, scores obtained by individuals from cultures other than mainstream American culture should be interpreted with caution. Moreover, since only a limited number of intellectual abilities are sampled by these tests, the examiner should be careful about predicting performance in situations where other abilities may be more important for success.

Intelligence tests were originally devised to predict school achievement and this is still the most valid use of these tests today. Matarazzo (1972) reviewed a number of studies exploring the relationship between IQ scores and school performance and concluded that the correlation between them is about .50. Sattler (1972) reported that the median correlation between WISC Full Scale IQ and measures of academic achievement was about .60. This level of correlation indicates that IQ scores can provide useful information for the prediction of school achievement, but by no means do they reflect all the relevant factors.

The information obtained from the administration of an intelligence test is also commonly used for personality assessment purposes. The assessment process can be viewed as a structured interview that allows the examiner to observe, under standard conditions, the work behavior and interpersonal interactions of the adolescent. Personality variables such as interpersonal warmth, impulsivity, and frustration tolerance can be directly observed.

Moreover, the actual responses to items may reveal important attitudes, preoccupations, or idiosyncratic viewpoints. A more controversial method involves the use of subtest profiles for the identification of certain personality types. For example, adolescent delinquents have been reported to have Performance IQ scores significantly higher than Verbal IQ scores, with Picture Arrangement and Object Assembly being relatively elevated and Information and Comprehension being relatively depressed (Goldstein & Hersen, 1984).

THE WECHSLER SCALES

The Wechsler scales (WISC-R & WAIS-R) are the most widely used individually administered tests for the assessment of the intellectual functioning of adolescents. The Wechsler Intelligence Scale for Children-Revised (WISC-R) was published in 1974 and is used for the assessment of individuals aged 6 through 16 years. The Wechsler Adult Intelligence Scale-Revised (WAIS-R) was published in 1981 and has norms for the assessment of individuals aged 16 through 74 years. The WISC-R comprises five verbal subtests, five performance subtests, and two supplemental subtests, one for each scale. The WAIS-R has six verbal subtests and five performance subtests. Both tests yield Verbal, Performance, and Full Scale IQ scores. The popularity of the Wechsler scales is due in great part to the availability of these three summary scores and the subtest structure which allows for the assessment of a variety of cognitive skills. The means of the IQ scores were set at 100 with standard deviations of 15. The subtest scaled scores have a means of 10 and standard deviations of 3.

The reliabilities of the IQ scores for both tests are quite high. The average WISC-R split-half reliability is .96 for the Full Scale IQ, .94 for the Verbal IQ, and .90 for the Performance IQ. The corresponding reliabilities for the WAIS-R are .97, .97, and .93. Test–retest reliabilities for WAIS-R in the 25 to 34 year-old-age group are .95 for the Full Scale IQ, .94 for the Verbal IQ, and .89 for the Performance IQ. The corresponding reliabilities for the $14\frac{1}{2}$ to $15\frac{1}{2}$-year-old age group on the WISC-R are .95, .95, and .89. The reliabilities for the individual subtests are generally not as high. Split-half reliabilities for the subtests of the WISC-R averaged over all age groups range from .70 for Object Assembly to .89 for Vocabulary. Test–retest reliabilities for $14\frac{1}{2}$ to $15\frac{1}{2}$ year old range from .50 for Mazes to .88 for Information. Corresponding reliabilities for the WAIS-R are somewhat higher.

When an individual is retested with the WISC-R after a one or two month period, the average gain on retesting is $3\frac{1}{2}$ points on the Verbal Scale, $9\frac{1}{2}$ points on the Performance Scale, and 7 points on the Full Scale (Wechsler, 1974). On the WAIS-R the gain is approximately the same.

Although the Wechsler scales provide scores on a number of subtests, these tend to be highly intercorrelated and factor analytic studies suggest that only two or three factors account for much of the variance in the scores. Thus the tests do not adequately cover the domain of intelligent behaviors; in fact, the items appear to be mostly related to school achievement (Hale, 1983). The Wechsler scales also have the disadvantage of not discriminating well at the high and low ends of the IQ range (ie. below 40 and above 160). If a client is thought to fall at the extremes of the spectrum, the examiner should consider using the Stanford-Binet test, which has more floor and ceiling.

The WAIS-R and WISC-R overlap at the 16-year level, and either test is appropriate for assessing this age group. Unlike the older WAIS, the WAIS-R yields IQ scores that are very close (within one or two points on average) to those obtained on the WISC-R. If a 16-year-old has been recently or frequently tested with the WISC-R, the examiner should consider using the WAIS-R to attenuate the effects of retesting.

TESTING ADOLESCENTS

When conducting an intellectual assessment, it is important to obtain at least the client's average or typical performance so that the scores will be valid estimates of current functioning. Adolescents almost never refer themselves for an evaluation, and they may come to the testing session in an angry and mistrustful frame of mind making this task difficult. The examiner needs to make a conscious effort to establish rapport before administering an IQ test. It is helpful in this regard to adopt a friendly but direct and businesslike manner. The session can begin with a brief discussion of the reasons for the assessment and the nature of the tests. The advantages of an accurate evaluation should be mentioned in an effort to engage the adolescent's self-interest. The test may be described as a series of tasks, both verbal and nonverbal, which start out easy and become progressively more difficult. The subject should be instructed to work hard even on the most difficult items. Descriptions of the test as fun or gamelike should be avoided.

It is usually worthwhile to spend some time in informal conversation with the adolescent. Non-threatening questions about the individual's age, grade placement, favorite and least liked subjects, family composition, hobbies, and career goals can be woven into the conversation. More probing and confrontational interviewing should be conducted after all the testing has been completed. This allows the examiner to follow up on information gathered during the test administration and allows the examiner to be more confrontational without jeopardizing the intellectual assessment itself.

Wechsler (1974) suggests that the examiner reward effort throughout the evaluation but at no time indicate whether a response was correct or not. If the adolescent gives flippant or negativistic answers, these should not be scored as errors without further probing. For example if the adolescent says there are no reasons to have police officers, the examiner can say, "Well, try to give me some answers that other people might think reasonable" (p. 56).

THE INTERPRETATION OF THE WECHSLER SCALES

Sattler (1982) advocates a five-step approach to the interpretation of the Wechsler scales. The first step is to consider the implications of the Full Scale IQ score.

FULL SCALE IQ

The Full Scale IQ is the most reliable of Wechsler scores and can be interpreted with the most confidence. It provides the best estimate of the individual's overall intellectual functioning and allows for a determination of the adolescent's standing relative to same-aged peers. All other scores should be viewed in the context of the Full Scale IQ. Further analysis of the Wechsler scales is primarily an attempt to carve the Full Scale score into components that will provide a more meaningful description of the individual's intellectual functioning.

VERBAL SCALE AND PERFORMANCE SCALE DIFFERENCES

The next step in this process involves an examination of the Performance Scale and Verbal Scale IQ scores. The Verbal Scale is considered a measure of verbal comprehension abilities, while the Performance Scale is a measure of perceptual organizational abilities. The Full Scale IQ score may mask significant differences in these two areas. A 12 point difference between the Verbal and Performance Scales is significant at the .05 level on the average for the WISC-R while a 10 point difference is significant at that level on the WAIS-R. On both tests, a difference of 15 points is considered to be important and worthy of further investigation.

Although reflecting meaningful differences in a person's cognitive abilities, significant Verbal–Performance discrepancies should not automatically be interpreted as indicative of abnormality. A discrepancy of 15 points on the WISC-R is found in 24% of a normal sample and is therefore not unusual. A Verbal–Performance difference of 25 points, however, occurs in only 5% of a normal population (Kaufman, 1979) and warrants further exploration.

The Verbal and Performance scales only approximate the Verbal Comprehension and Perceptual Organization factors as revealed by factor-analytic studies of the Wechsler scales. Kaufman's (1975) analysis showed Information, Similarities, Vocabulary, and Comprehension to load on the Verbal

Comprehension factor, while Picture Completion, Picture Arrangement, Block Design, and Object Assembly loaded on the Perceptual Organization factor. A third factor labeled Freedom from Distractibility was formed by the Arithmetic, Digit Span, and Coding subtests.

Gutkin (1978) presents formulas for the computation of deviation quotients for the Verbal Comprehension and Perceptual Organization factors of the WISC-R. These quotients are comparable to IQ scores and have a mean of 100 and a standard deviation of 15. The verbal comprehension deviation quotient (VCDQ) is given by the formula:

$$VCDQ = 1.47 \ (I + S + V + C) + 41.2$$

I,S,V, and C are the scaled scores of the corresponding verbal subtests. The perceptual organization deviation quotient (PODQ) is given by:

$$PODQ = 1.6 \ (PC + PA + BD + OA) + 36$$

Sattler (1982) gives this formula for the Freedom from Distractibility factor:

$$FDDQ = 2.2 \ (A + DS + Co) + 34.0$$

Calculation of these scores can help in the interpretation of the Freedom from Distractibility factor and in the interpretation of the other two factors in those situations where an inspection of the subtest scores suggests that the Verbal and/or Performance Scale IQs are not good approximations of the Verbal Comprehension or Perceptual Organization factors. In general, if Arithmetic, Digit Span, or Coding is significantly discrepant ($+/-3$ scaled score points) from the mean of the subtests making up their respective IQ scale (Verbal or Performance) and the other components of the Freedom from Distractibility factor are in the same direction (i.e., above or below the mean), it is usually worthwhile to compute all three factor scores for purposes of interpretation. If the components of the Freedom from Distractibility factor are not discrepant from their scale means, then interpretations can be based on the Verbal and Performance Scale IQ scores (Kaufman, 1979).

Intersubtest Scatter

The third step in the process of interpretation is the analysis of intersubtest scatter. Kaufman (1979) provides a detailed discussion of this step. He recommends that the mean scaled score be calculated for the Verbal and Performance scales separately. Then each subtest scaled score is compared to its respective scaled score mean. Subtests that are three or more points higher then their mean are considered measures of significant cognitive strengths, while those that are 3 or more points below their mean are considered to reflect significant cognitive weaknesses. The examiner's next task is to make sense out of any resulting pattern of strengths and weaknesses by considering all the possible abilities that could contribute to success or failure on the

Table 6.1. Abilities and Factors Affecting Subtest Performance

Subtest	Abilities and Factors
Information	• Fund of accumulated factual information • Remote memory • Alertness to environment • School learning
Similarities	• Verbal concept formation • Logical abstract reasoning • Facility of verbal expression
Arithmetic	• Numerical reasoning ability • Concentration and mental alertness • Anxiety and distractibility • School learning
Vocabulary	• Verbal intelligence and learning ability • Word knowledge and verbal expression • Fund of information • Educational and cultural experiences
Comprehension	• Social judgment and common sense • Verbal reasoning and expression • Practical knowledge and awareness • Moral sense
Digit Span	• Immediate auditory memory • Attention span • Number facility • Anxiety and distractibility
Picture Completion	• Awareness of environmental details • Concentration and visual alertness • Ability to differentiate essential from nonessential details
Picture Arrangement	• Ability to comprehend a total situation • Perception of cause and effect relationships • Social intelligence and planning ability • Cultural background
Block Design	• Perceptual organization and visual–motor coordination • Nonverbal concept formation • Reproduction of models • Effort and concentration
Object Assembly	• Visual–motor coordination and perceptual organization • Synthesis • Flexibility • Perception of relationships among parts
Coding/Digit Symbol	• Psychomotor speed • Visual–motor coordination • Learning ability • Integrated brain functioning • Anxiety and distractibility

subtests in question. Table 6.1 presents some of the abilities associated with each subtest.

Kaufman (1979) and others (Sattler, 1972) who discuss the analysis of subtest profiles are careful to point out that this exercise should be used to generate hypotheses about an individual's functioning, and should not be used for decisions such as classification or placement. This should be kept in mind, since profile analysis is a controversial practice and subject to misuse. Hirshoren and Kavale (1976) have argued that the relatively low reliabilities of the WAIS-R subtests preclude valid profile analyses. Hale (1983) commented that although research in this area has shown profile differences between well defined groups of subjects, these profiles are not distinctive enough to allow the accurate classification of an individual. He concluded that knowledge of a person's subtest profile by itself does not allow the clinician to accurately predict either academic achievement levels or behavioral problems. Therefore, interpretations based on subtest patterns should be considered tentative until corroborated by other data.

It is also important to consider the amount of intersubtest scatter in a person's performance on the Wechsler scales. This can be measured simply by calculating the difference between the highest and lowest subtest scores. Kaufman (1979) reports that in the WISC-R standardization sample, the average scatter was 7 with a standard deviation of 2 points. Thus a considerable amount of subtest scatter is to be expected in a normal record. Kaufman suggests that scatter of 10 points can be reported as "substantial," while scatter of 12 or more points is needed before questions of abnormality can be considered.

Intrasubtest Scatter

The next step in the process of interpretation proposed by Sattler (1982) is an examination of intrasubtest scatter. This refers to the pattern of success and failures within a particular subtest. It is normal for a subject to pass the easy items and then to fail progressively more of the difficult ones. The pattern of failing easy items while succeeding on more difficult ones may indicate attentional problems or difficulty establishing a response set. This latter problem is seen in individuals who are slow to catch on to a task, but once they have, perform quite well.

The final step in the interpretive process is a qualitative analysis of the actual content of the subject's responses to the Information, Vocabulary, Comprehension, and Similarities subtests. The examiner should be alert for responses indicating aggressive tendencies or antisocial attitudes. Are there any unusual associations or overly personalized responses that might suggest psychopathology? Are word finding problems evident? Are responses very concrete in nature? Does the content of any of the responses suggest an overly passive attitude toward life?

When an intellectual assessment is conducted with a clear understanding of its strengths and limitations, it can contribute valuable information to the understanding of an adolescent's cognitive, personality, vocational, and academic functioning.

TESTS OF ACADEMIC ACHIEVEMENT

The assessment of academic functioning is often an important part of the comprehensive psychological assessment of an adolescent client. When combined with measures of cognitive functioning, the information from an academic assessment can answer questions concerning academic underachievement, learning disabilities, or readiness for post-secondary education.

A seemingly sudden deterioration in an adolescent's school performance will frequently occasion a referral for psychological evaluation, and in such cases the inclusion of an academic assessment can aid in determining the nature of the difficulty. If a relatively recent event, such as involvement in drug use or an emergent psychiatric condition, is central to the problem, then a picture of academic skills uniformly developed to near grade level can be expected. If a pattern of spotty and unsystematic skill acquisition is demonstrated, a more chronic emotional or behavioral disorder may be indicated. However, if a specific academic deficit is revealed, the examiner should be alerted to the possibility that a previously unrecognized learning disability may be contributing to the current school problems.

Although most severe learning disorders will have been identified before adolescence, some cases will escape detection in childhood especially if the individual, by virtue of extraordinary effort or superior intellect, is able to achieve at grade level. Even in cases where learning disabilities are identified at an early age, reassessment in adolescence can explicate current patterns of skill development and suggest new educational goals.

Psychologists often include in their test batteries a brief measure of academic functioning, such as the Wide Range Achievement Test-Revised (Jastak & Wilkinson, 1984) or the Peabody Individual Achievement Test (Dunn & Markwardt, 1970). These tests serve a screening function by providing rough estimates of the individual's achievement level in a number of important subject areas. When a more extensive evaluation of the adolescent's academic functioning is needed, a more lengthy and comprehensive test, such as the Woodcock-Johnson Psycho-Educational Battery, Part II: Tests of Achievement (Woodcock & Johnson, 1977) should be considered. The Wide Range Achievement Test-Revised (WRAT-R) and the Woodcock-Johnson will be described below. Table 6.2 presents other individually administered achievement tests that can be used with adolescents.

WRAT-R

The WRAT-R is the newest version of the Wide Range Achievement Test first standardized in 1936 by Joseph Jastak. It provides measures of achievement in three areas: arithmetic computation, oral reading, and written

Table 6.2. Selected Educational Tests for use with Adolescents

Assessment	Age Range	Description
Peabody Individual Achievement Test	K–12	Assesses word recognition, reading comprehension, spelling, math, and general information. Administered individually.
Gray Oral Reading Test	1–12	Assesses competency of oral reading skills. Administered individually, provides descriptive and diagnostic information.
Woodcock Reading Mastery Tests	K–12	Contains 5 subtests assessing word identification, word comprehension, word attack, passage comprehension, and letter identification.
Kaufman Test of Educational Achievement	6 years–18 years 11 months	Contains a brief and a comprehensive form which assess reading decoding, reading comprehension, math application, math computation, and spelling. Age norms are compared with IQ scores and generate criteria for learning disabilites.
Test of Written Spelling	1–12	Assesses both regularly spelled words and those that follow an exception.

spelling. The WRAT has been popular with psychologists over the years because its brief (20–30 minutes) administration time made it easy to include in an assessment battery. However, it has also been criticized for inadequate normative sampling and the lack of test–retest reliability data, as well as measures of internal consistency.

The WRAT-R has attempted to address these problems. This edition is standardized on a stratified national sample of 5600 individuals — 200 in each of 28 age groups from 5 years, 0 months to 74 years, 11 months. Test–retest reliability coefficients are presented. For the adolescent age group, these are .90 for Reading, .89 for Spelling, and .79 for Arithmetic. Item and person separation indexes are presented as measures of internal consistency with median values for the adolescent age groups (12–19) ranging from .89 for the person separation index of the Arithmetic subtest to .99 for the item separation index of the Reading and Spelling subtests.

The WRAT-R is divided into two levels. Level 2 is for persons aged 12 years, 0 months through adulthood. The Reading subtest consists of recognizing and naming letters and reading words out of context. There is no attempt to measure reading comprehension. The Spelling subtest involves copying symbols that resemble letters, writing one's name, and writing words to dictation. The Arithmetic subtest consists of counting dots, reading numbers, solving oral math problems, and performing written computations. The simplest parts of each subtest are administered only if the subject does poorly on the main section.

The scores for the three subtests are reported separately. There is no total score. Standard scores, grade equivalents, and percentiles are usually reported. The standard scores have a mean of 100 and a standard deviation of

15, allowing comparisons with the Wechsler scales. If an individual's WRAT-R standard score falls approximately 15 points below their Full Scale IQ score, then the possibility of significant underachievement in that area should be considered. Moreover, because the WRAT-R is individually administered it provides an opportunity to observe the adolescent working on a sample of educational tasks. In this regard, it is useful to record verbatim the individual's attempts to pronounce the reading list and to examine their calculations on the arithmetic section for characteristic errors.

Woodcock-Johnson Psycho-Educational Battery

One of the most popular and commonly used educational assessment devices for adolescents is the Woodcock-Johnson Psycho-Educational Battery, Part II. The entire battery contains two separate units — Part I, which contains the cognitive clusters of tests, and Part II, which contains the achievement and interest clusters. The Tests of Achievement comprise 10 subtests covering the areas of reading, mathematics, written language, science, social science, and humanities. The subtests are: Letter-Word Identification, Word Attack, Passage Comprehension, Calculation, Applied Problems, Dictation, Proofing, Science, Social Science, and Humanities. When only the achievement tests are given, the administration takes from 30 to 60 minutes. Scoring takes an additional 10 to 15 minutes.

All the subtests except Word Attack and Proofing have rules for establishing both basal and ceiling items. Raw scores are all the items below the basal plus all the correct items between the basal and ceiling items. Cluster scores are constructed for Reading (Letter-Word Identification, Word attack, and Passage Comprehension); Mathematics (Calculation and Applied Problems); Written Language (Dictation and Proofing); and Knowledge (Science, Social Science, and Humanities). Grade equivalents, age equivalents and percentile rank scores are computed. A Relative Performance Index is also calculated which indicates the subject's expected level of performance at 90% mastery. This score is useful for planning instructional levels. In addition, several profiles can be drawn which aid in score interpretation.

The Woodcock-Johnson battery was standardized on a national sample, based on 1970 Census data, and covers the range of 3 to 65 years of age. Its psychometric qualities are generally considered good. Item difficulty for each subtest was calibrated using a Rasch model, and median reliabilities for subtests range from .83 to .95. This test is especially valuable because it samples a broad range of academic skills and knowledge areas. When combined with the results from an intellectual assessment, it can provide useful information concerning an individual's current educational functioning and need for remedial programming.

Chapter 7

Neuropsychological Assessment

Neuropsychological assessment has become increasingly popular as psychologists have begun to emphasize the importance of brain–behavior relationships in the comprehensive understanding of an individual's psychosocial functioning. This chapter will discuss some issues relevant to the neuropsychological assessment of adolescents and describe some tests and procedures appropriate for this population.

REASONS FOR REFERRAL

The most common questions occasioning the referral of an adolescent for neuropsychological assessment will vary from setting to setting. In educational settings, questions about learning disabilities are frequently encountered, while in an inpatient psychiatry unit, questions are often asked about the contribution of possible organic factors to an individual's pathology. In medical or surgical settings, neuropsychological assessment may be requested to monitor the course of illness or recovery from injury or neurosurgery.

Although psychologists do not make medical diagnoses, as neuropsychologists they are often asked to provide data and interpretations relevant to the diagnoses of organic impairment. Even when neurological dysfunction is well established, neuropsychological assessment may assist rehabilitation planning by explicating a client's pattern of cognitive strengths and weakness. With the advent of CAT scans and other advances in neurological assessment, the emphasis in neuropsychological testing has shifted from aiding diagnosis to helping rehabilitation. Still, there are cases where the CAT scan is not definitive and the results from a neuropsychological assessment are valuable in indicating the likelihood of neurological dysfunction.

In some instances, the categorization of an adolescent's problems as organic in nature may make an important contribution to his or her care. This is especially so in cases where an acute neurological condition lends itself to medical or surgical treatment. In other cases, the acknowledgment of underlying chronic organic impairment can provide the adolescent and his family with a more realistic understanding of the problem and avoid the frustrations and expense attendant upon viewing the problem as caused by laziness or an emotional disorder. However, in most instances the mere identification of an adolescent as neurologically impaired has little value. What is more helpful is a detailed description of the individual's mental and emotional functioning that furthers an understanding of his or her neurological status and provides information useful for rehabilitation. Given this fact, the practice of using a few tests to "screen" for brain damage is usually inappropriate.

THE USE OF SCREENING TESTS

The purpose of screening is to identify, by the use of economically administered tests or procedures, those individuals in a population who need further evaluation to determine the presence of a particular condition. Screening for brain damage was a fairly popular notion in the 1940s and 1950s when a more unitary view of brain damage held sway (Lezak, 1983). However, it is now generally understood that brain damage is a very heterogeneous concept, and that injury to one part of the brain may not impair the same cognitive functions as damage to another area of the brain or impair cognitive functions in any obvious way at all.

A test of a rather specific function, such as the Bender Gestalt test (Bender, 1938), may be insensitive to lesions in areas of the brain not directly related to visual–motor functioning. If, on the other hand, a screening test taps a broad range of mental abilities, it is likely to be affected by psychiatric and situational disturbances, as well as brain dysfunction. Thus, screening procedures tend to produce false positives and false negatives at rates that compromise their use with individual clients. In general, screening procedures should be used only on a population-wide basis. When a referral for an individual evaluation includes questions of a neuropsychological nature, a more extensive neuropsychological evaluation is usually required. Of course it should be kept in mind that even an extensive evaluation cannot rule out the possibility of organic impairment. The most the examiner can state is that no evidence of impairment was found on the measures used.

DEVELOPMENTAL CONSIDERATIONS AND FRONTAL LOBE DYSFUNCTION

Older adolescents are cognitively more mature than younger adolescents, and these developmental differences must be taken into account when conducting a neuropsychological assessment. In general, neuropsychological measures developed for adults can be cautiously used with individuals 15 years old and older, while with younger youths one should use instruments specifically designed and normed for this age group. In all cases, developmental issues need to be taken into account when interpreting test results. Of particular relevance in this regard is the maturation of the frontal lobes during adolescents and the emergence of the intellectual functions associated with them.

The frontal lobes are not fully mature until late adolescents and often not until 21 years of age for males. Because of this, damage to the frontal lobes incurred in early childhood or even *in utero* may not become evident until adolescence. Moreover, adolescence is a time when an individual, especially a male, is at increased risk for a closed head injury, which often results in damage to the frontal lobes either through a blow to the front of the head or through a *countre-coup* injury which occurs when a blow to the rear of the head results in the brain being driven against the front of the skull. Unfortunately, damage to the frontal lobes is not easily assessed.

With the exception of the Wisconsin Card Sorting Test discussed below, few instruments purport to assess frontal lobe functions. These functions tend to be qualitative in nature, and damage to the frontal lobes does not usually result in obvious cognitive impairment. Rather, the impairment may be revealed in the course of day-to-day living as poor judgment and planning ability, disinhibition, impulsivity, and reduced responsiveness to social conventions. The patient may exhibit a loss of initiative and a concrete mental attitude, making it difficult to shift sets and adjust to new situations. Moreover, the individual may appear careless, socially inappropriate, and crude. Of course, poor planning and socially inappropriate behaviors are not uncommon for adolescents, and the determination of frontal lobe dysfunction requires an understanding of the full range of normal adolescent behavior, as well as the symptoms associated with frontal lobe lesions.

Normal Variability

A major consideration in the assessment of all age groups, including adolescents, is the considerable amount of asymmetry in the human brain, resulting in considerable variation in patterns of cognitive abilities within a normal population. The mere presence of wide discrepancies in an individual's cognitive abilities is not in itself indicative of neurological impairment. What is indicative are patterns of strengths and weaknesses that conform to patterns known to be associated with specific types of dysfunction. For example, verbal abilities significantly below performance abilities, when added to right sided motor weakness in a right-handed individual, is more suggestive of left hemisphere pathology than a verbal–performance discrepancy alone. However, even in cases where pathology is not indicated, wide discrepancies in cognitive skills may have important implications for educational and vocational planning.

Learning Disabilities

Most obvious developmental and learning disabilities will have been identified by the time an individual reaches adolescence, and the role of neuropsychological assessment at this age is more concerned with remediation than diagnosis. For young adolescents, the emphasis may be on academic programming, while for older adolescents career goals and vocational planning become more central (Hartlage and Telzrow, 1986). Neuropsychological assessment should reveal the global level of intellectual functioning, any relative difficulty in processing verbal as opposed to spatial information, and specific strengths or weaknesses in a broad range of perceptual, cognitive and motor functions. The neuropsychologist then uses his or her knowledge of teaching techniques and job requirements to translate these data into meaningful recommendations.

Remediation

In general, adolescents do not respond as well as children to direct attempts to remediate deficits, and individuals of any age with neurological dysfunction may be unduly frustrated by repeated attempts to directly teach them a skill they lack the prerequisite abilities to perform. Therefore, for most adolescents the educational intervention model developed by Hartlage and Telzrow (1983), the "capitalization of strengths continuum", is appropriate. On one end of the continuum, for the milder forms of learning disabilities, strength matched teaching is recommended, which attempts to use the adolescent's identified neuropsychological strengths to circumvent deficits and teach basic academic skills. For example, the psychologist might recommend, on the basis of neuropsychological testing, that reading instruction should emphasize the visuo–spatial features of words, as opposed to a more phonetic approach. On the other end of the continuum are individuals with very severe learning disabilities who are unable to learn academic skills beyond a rudimentary level. For such individuals, recommendations are made for the use of compensatory techniques to assist with the acquisition of functional life skills — for example, the use of bus tokens to avoid the need to count change.

BEGINNING THE ASSESSMENT

The neuropsychological evaluation begins with the stated referral questions from which the examiner begins to form a set of more specific and answerable questions that will guide the investigation. Using his or her knowledge of neuropathology, assessment techniques, adolescent psychology, and the referral source, the examiner will often expand and modify the original questions in order to produce a more complete and useful report. For example, knowing that adolescence is often a transitional period to the world of work, an examiner may explore the vocational implications of the youth's cognitive strengths and weaknesses, even though this was not specifically requested.

The next step is for the examiner to collect enough background information to form a context within which to interpret test findings. It is usually important to ascertain if the adolescent's current level of functioning represents a deterioration from a previously higher level, and, if so, when the deterioration became evident. A careful medical and developmental history is important in this regard, with special attention to development milestones and the occurrence of risk factors such as high fever or head trauma. An interview with the parents can provide this information, as well as data on the adolescent's current situation and daily living skills. A review of school records is also helpful in establishing prior level of functioning and pattern of academic abilities. Of course, previous psychological test scores should be noted. After collecting this information, the examiner is in a position to decide on the scope of the evaluation and the measures to be used. The extent to which personality factors need to be assessed should be decided and consideration given to the adolescent's actual age.

EXPANDING THE SCOPE OF THE EVALUATION

It is often necessary to include a formal evaluation of the adolescent's personality functioning. This is especially important when an attempt is being made to differentiate between organic and functional etiology. Likewise, it is important to explicate any emotional problems which may be secondary to the cognitive dysfunction, such as poor self-image, depression, or specific anxieties. An understanding of the adolescent's personality style is also helpful when formulating recommendations. Personality measures such as the MMPI, TAT, or Rorschach can be helpful in this regard.

An interview with the adolescent can also provide valuable information and should not be omitted. It is often useful to inquire directly about the adolescent's experience of the presenting problems. What situations or tasks cause the youth the greatest problems, and how does he or she cope with them? What is the adolescent's attitude toward his or her difficulties? Does he or she have any problems with eating or sleeping, or any headaches or strange sensations? Inquire about how their stated problems affect their school performance, extracurricular activities, hobbies, social life, family relations, and plans for the future.

It is also important to make careful behavioral observations throughout the evaluation, including the observation of any physical abnormalities, since these may be associated with underlying organic impairment. The examiner should be alert for signs of visual or auditory impairment, fine or gross motor difficulties, word finding problems, variations in level of awareness, or marked distractibility. The examiner should also pay close attention to how the patient attempts to solve various problems, especially those with which they have difficulty. The examiner should attempt to observe where in the processing of the task the breakdown occurs. Why an item is failed is often more important than the fact that it was failed.

Moreover, how the adolescent relates to the examiner, reacts to frustrations and failures, and approaches difficult tasks should be noted, since these may have important implications for how the adolescent functions in settings such as work or school. The subtle deficits of a frontal lobe syndrome, such as lack of initiative, deficient self-criticism, or blunted social sensibility may reveal themselves as qualitative aspects of the adolescent's behavior, as opposed to any specific patterns of test scores.

SELECTING BATTERIES OR SPECIFIC TESTS

There are two main approaches to the selection of the tests to be used in a neuropsychological assessment. In the first approach the examiner administers a standard battery of tests, such as the Halstead-Reitan Neuropsychological Battery, to all cases. This is the traditional approach and it has several advantages. It assures a comprehensive review of functions for all subjects with well standardized procedures, and it allows interpretations to be based on well-established patterns of performance. The limited set of procedures can be learned relatively easily, and with constant practice the examiner becomes very proficient with their administration. On the other hand, the use of a standard battery for all individuals can be inefficient in cases where the information from all tests is not needed, and inflexible in cases where additional tests are required to fully answer the referral questions.

The second approach involves the use of a flexible battery where tests are selected on an individual case-by-case basis. Often a core battery of tests is administered to most cases, with additional tests used as needed to address the referral questions or test hypotheses developed during the evaluation. This approach requires the examiner to have knowledge of a wide range of assessment procedures, as well as a sophisticated understanding of neuropsychology. And there is the further drawback that a functional deficit may be overlooked. However, the increased efficiency of this methodology and its potential for the more meaningful assessment of an individual case make it highly attractive to many neuropsychologists.

AA—F

The Reitan Batteries

The Reitan-Indian Neuropsychological Battery for Children is a downward extension of the Halstead-Reitan Neuropsychological Battery which is widely used with adults. There are two separate versions, one for younger children (5–8) and one for older children (9–14). The version for older children is appropriate for use with young adolescents, while the adult version can be used with adolescents aged 15 and above.

The Halstead-Reitan Battery consists of five core tests: the Category Test, the Tactual Performance Test, the Rhythm Test, the Speech Sounds Perception Test, and the Finger Oscillation Test (Finger Tapping Test). These five tests yield seven measures, which are used to calculate an Impairment Index that provides an overall measure of performance and a cutoff score for the identification of brain damage.

Additional tests in the battery are the Trail Making Test, Strength of Grip Test, Modified Halstead-Wepman Aphasia Screening Test, Sensory-Perceptual Examination, Tactile Perception, one of the Wechsler intelligence tests, and the Minnesota Multiphasic Personality Inventory. It takes from five to eight hours to administer the complete battery, depending on the degree of impairment.

The battery is analysed by way of Reitan's four "methods of inference". First, the overall level of performance is examined by looking at the Impairment Index in relation to the cutting score. Second, the presence of pathognomonic signs is noted. A pathognomonic sign is one that occurs rarely in a population, but, when it does occur, is almost always indicative of neurological impairment. Examples are the inability to identify a familiar object or perform a simple drawing task. Third, the pattern of performance on the various tests is examined for indications of the type and location of the lesion. Finally, sensory, perceptual, and motor functions on the right and left sides of the body are compared. Impaired performance on only one side of the body is suggestive of both the presence of brain damage and the laterality of the lesion.

The Halstead-Reitan test batteries are particularly well suited for research purposes and have demonstrated their ability to reliably identify individuals with brain damage (Lezak, 1983). However they are also costly, time-consuming, relatively non-portable, and deficient in their assessment of memory functions.

The Luria–Nebraska Battery

Another popular battery is the Luria–Nebraska Neuropsychological Battery (Golden, Hammeke, & Purisch, 1980) which was developed in an attempt to standardize and validate the clinical method of the Soviet neuropsychologist A. R. Luria. Golden and his colleagues took test items from the manual written by Christensen (1975) detailing the materials and procedures utilized by Luria and evaluated their ability to discriminate between normal subjects and a group of neurologically impaired patients. Items selected in this manner were assigned to eleven scales based on the original content groupings of Christensen, with the exception of Reading and Writing, which form separate scales in Golden's battery. Three additional scales are derived from selected items of the other scales: The Pathognomonic, Right Hemisphere, and Left Hemisphere scales. The eleven content scales are: Motor Functions, Rhythm and Pitch, Tactile and Kinesthetic Function, Visual Function, Receptive Language, Expressive Language, Reading, Writing, Arithmetic, Memory, and Intelligence.

The Lurian-Nebraska Neuropsychological Battery provides a relatively brief assessment of a number of sensory, motor, and intellectual functions. It has been shown to discriminate between normal control subjects and neurologically impaired patients (Golden, Hammeke, & Purisch, 1978; Hammeke, Golden, & Purisch, 1978) and between brain-damaged and schizophrenic subjects (Purisch, Golden, & Hammeke, 1978). However it has been criticized on both theoretical and psychometric grounds. It is not a comprehensive battery, lacking tests of attention, concentration, and mental tracking, as well as fund of information. Its extensive use of time limits makes it difficult to separate the effects of generalized mental slowing from the impairment of specific functions (Lezak, 1983), and the overlapping content of the scales makes the interpretation of any given scale ambiguous (Spiers, 1981). Spiers also makes the point that, although the battery consists of test items developed by A. R. Luria, it does not duplicate his method of using them to test hypotheses concerning the various abilities, deficits, or functions of an individual patient.

THE INDIVIDUALIZED BATTERY APPROACH

The use of an individualized battery requires the examiner to be knowledgeable about a wide range of assessment procedures and to choose those procedures that will be most appropriate in a particular case. An important resource for the neuropsychologist interested in this approach is Muriel Lezak's book *Neuropsychological Assessment* (1983), which presents a detailed discussion of the theory and practice of neuropsychological assessment, as well as a compendium of tests and assessment techniques.

Many neuropsychologists who use an individualized battery have a core group of tests that they give to most cases. These tests should provide a fairly comprehensive review of basic cognitive functions utilizing both verbal and nonverbal modalities. Table 7.1 presents these basic functional areas and a few selected methods of assessment. It should be noted that a number of these

Table 7.1. Cognitive Functions and Some Related Measures

Function	Test
Verbal	
Language Skills	• WISC-R Vocabulary subtest
	• Peabody Picture Vocabulary Test
	• WRAT-R Reading subtest
	• Modified Halstead-Wepman Aphasia Screening Test
Reasoning and Judgment	• WISC-R Comprehension subtest
	• WISC-R Similarities subtest
Arithmetic	• WISC-R Arithmetic subtest
	• WRAT-R Arithmetic subtest
Nonverbal	• WISC-R Picture Completion subtest
Ideation and Reasoning	• WISC-R Picture Arrangement subtest
	• Raven Progressive Matrices
	• Wisconsin Card Sort Test
Visuo-practic	• Bender-Gestalt Test
	• WISC-R Block Design subtest
	• WISC-R Object Assembly subtest
	• Draw-A-Person
	• WISC-R Mazes subtest
Memory	
Immediate	• WISC-R Digit Span (forward)
	• Auditory-Verbal Learning Test (I & B)
	• Benton Visual Retention Test
Short Term	• Auditory-Verbal Learning Test (II-VI)
Remote	• WISC-R Information subtest
Attention/Concentration/	• Symbol Digits Modalities Test
Tracking	• WISC-R Coding subtest
	• Trail Making Test
	• WISC-R Digit Span (backwards)
	• WISC-R Arithmetic subtest
Motor	• Purdue Pegboard Test
	• Finger Tapping Test
Somatosensory	• Single and Double Simultaneous Stimulation Test

tests are neither purely verbal nor nonverbal in nature but depend on both verbal and nonverbal cognitive processes for success. The Picture Completion subtest of the WISC-R, for example, is listed as a nonverbal procedure but requires verbal responses to visual stimuli. Moreover, a test may tap more than one functional area within a modality. For example, the Arithmetic subtest of the WISC-R is listed under both Arithmetic and the Attention/Concentration/Tracking areas, since both are measured by this test. Therefore the interpretation of any one test depends on a consideration of the subject's performance on other tests in the battery. Several tests that are appropriate for the neuropsychological assessment of adolescents are discussed below.

The Raven Progressive Matrices

The Raven Progressive Matrices (Raven, 1960) is an easily administered test of visuospatial reasoning consisting of 60 items grouped into five sets of

12 each. In the first set, the subject is presented a design with a part missing and is instructed to choose from six alternatives the one that completes the figure. This set appears to require the visuospatial abilities often associated with right hemisphere functioning. The next five sets consist of progressively more difficult analogy problems that require the subject to choose from up to eight alternatives the one that fits into the visually presented relationship. These items may depend more heavily upon left hemisphere functions (Denes et al., 1978). Although lesions in either hemisphere may result in subnormal scores on this test, the more marked the subnormality the greater the likelihood of right hemisphere involvement. Norms exist for ages 6 to 65.

Raven's Coloured Progressive Matrices (Raven, 1965) is a simplified 36-item adaptation of the standard matrices for children in the $5\frac{1}{2}$ to 11-year-old age range. Since proportionately more of the items of this version test visuospatial skills, this form is used by some neuropsychologists as a better measure of right hemisphere functioning.

The Symbol Digit Modalities Test

The Symbol Digit Modalities Test is a brief symbol substitution task that has been shown to be sensitive to organic impairment in both adults and children (Smith, 1973). The test is similar to the Wechsler Digit Symbol subtest except that the matching is the converse, requiring the subject to substitute numbers for symbols. This format is not only more difficult since the stimulus array is not in an orderly sequence, but it also allows for both written and oral responses to be given. This permits the testing of subjects with manual motor handicaps. Both oral and written administrations should be given when possible to provide for comparisons between the two response modalities.

A significant difference in the performance of one modality relative to the other points to a dysfunction of that modality. Subnormal scores on both administrations may reflect impairment of visual perception, visual scanning, oculomotor coordination, or general mental or motor slowing. Smith (1973) presents norms for children aged 8 to 17 while Centofanti (1975) has collected normative data on adults 18 to 74 years old. Smith (1973) considers scores more than 1.5 standard deviations below the subject's age norm to be "indicative" of cerebral dysfunction and scores 1 to 1.5 standard deviations below the mean age norm to be "suggestive".

The Wisconsin Card Sorting Test

The Wisconsin Card Sorting Test (Berg, 1948; Heaton, 1981) is a simple test of both concept formation and the ability to shift sets. The test consists of a pack of 64 cards on which are pictured one to four symbols: stars, triangles, crosses, or circles in red, green, yellow, or blue (i.e., 4 symbols x 4 colors x 4 numbers = 64 unique cards). Four stimulus cards are displayed — one red triangle, two green stars, three yellow crosses, and four blue circles — and the patient's task is to place one card under each stimulus, according to a principle that the patient must deduce from the examiner's feedback concerning the correctness of each response. For example, if the principle is "number" and the patient places a card with one green cross under the first stimulus card, the examiner responds with "right". If the category is "form", the correct placement of a star is under the stimulus "two green stars", regardless of the number or color of the stars on the card.

Most normal subjects catch on to the underlying principle with only a few errors. After the subject makes a run of 10 correct placements in a row, the examiner changes the principle by changing his or her verbal response to the subject's card placements. This change in feedback is the subject's only indication that a new category is being used and a shift in response set is required. The test begins with color as the correct category, shifts to form, then to number, and then repeats this sequence until the subject completes six runs of 10 correct placements each or demonstrates an inability to perform the task by placing all 64 cards without a run of 10 correct.

Scoring is usually done by counting the number of categories achieved (up to 6), perseverative errors, and either other or total errors. Perseverative errors occur when the patient sorts a card on the basis of the previously correct principle. This type of error reflects difficulty in forming concepts, utilizing feedback, and shifting response sets. Patients with frontal lobe dysfunction are especially prone to this type of error.

The PPVT-R

The Peabody Picture Vocabulary Test-Revised (Dunn, 1981) is a simple-to-administer test of vocabulary that requires the subject to pick the one picture out of four alternatives that correctly depicts the word spoken by the examiner. Since either pointing or giving the number of the picture is all that is required, individuals with expressive language difficulties are not unduly handicapped on this test. Norms are provided for individuals from $2\frac{1}{2}$ to 18-years-old and the test has a fairly high ceiling allowing for the detection of superior receptive vocabulary skills. Although an IQ score can be obtained, it is best to interpret it as a specific measure of receptive vocabulary as opposed to an estimate of more global intellectual functioning. Including this test in a neuropsychological assessment battery provides a good measure of verbal functioning independent of verbal expression.

The Auditory-Verbal Learning Test

The Auditory-Verbal Learning Test (Rey, 1964; Taylor, 1959) is a useful test of auditory-verbal memory that provides for an assessment of immediate memory span, learning over trials, and recall following an intervening activity. The examiner reads the subject a list of 15 words and the subject repeats as many of the words as possible directly after the list is presented (trial I). This provides a measure of immediate memory span for verbal material. The examiner then presents the same list for four additional trials (trials II-V) with the subject recalling as many words as possible each time. The number of words recalled on these trials yield a measure of the subject's verbal learning ability. The examiner then reads a new list of 15 words (trial B), which provides a second index of immediate recall and acts as an intervening activity. The subject is then asked to again recall the first list of words (trial IV).

Rey (1964) presents norms for adults and data on the performance of children and adolescents for trials I through V. Lezak (1983) collected data on the performance of normal and brain damaged patients on trial VI. She suggests that individuals whose recall drops by more than three words on trial VI compared to trial V probably have significant retention or retrieval problems.

The Benton Visual Retention Test

The Benton Visual Retention Test is a popular measure of visual memory and visual–motor abilities that is sensitive to the presence of organic impairment (Benton, 1974). There are three forms of approximate equivalence that can be used for repeated testing and four methods of administration. In Administration A, each of ten designs is presented for ten seconds and the patient is instructed to draw the design immediately afterward. Administration B uses a five-second exposure to each card. Administration C is a simple copying task, where the subject is presented each design and asked to draw it as accurately as possible. Administration D presents the designs for ten seconds but then requires the subject to delay 15 seconds before drawing them from memory. Benton provides adult norms for Administrations A, B, and C, and norms for children ages 8 through 14 for Administrations A and C.

Scores are calculated for number of correct designs and number of errors. Norms are broken down by both age and estimated premorbid IQ and it is easy to determine if either score falls into the impaired range.

The Purdue Pegboard Test

The Purdue Pegboard Test (Purdue Research Foundation, 1948) is a measure of manual dexterity that has proven useful in both the prediction of brain damage and the lateralization of lesions among brain damaged patients (Costa et al., 1963). The board has 50 holes in two parallel lines of 25 each and

50 small metal pegs. Four round depressions at the top of the board hold the pegs. The subject is instructed to pick up the pegs one at a time and place them in line as quickly as possible. The patient is tested with both the right and left hands alone and then using both hands simultaneously. Goldberg and Smith (1976) present cutoff scores for an administration procedure that includes two 30 second trials and one 60 second trial for each of the test conditions — preferred hand, nonpreferred hand, and simultaneous. Cutoff scores are reported for age groupings ranging from 5 to 70 years old. Four decision rules are presented for using these scores in the determination of brain damage and its possible lateralization.

The Single and Double Simultaneous Stimulation Test

The Single and Double Simultaneous Stimulation Test (Centofanti & Smith, 1979) is a brief test of somatosensory functions similar to the type often included in neurological examinations. Patients are instructed to close their eyes and place their hands on their knees. The examiner explains that he or she is going to touch the patient and the patient is to indicate, by pointing, where they were touched. The examiner delivers either single or simultaneous strokes with the index finger(s) to the patient's cheek(s) and/or back of hand(s). For example, the first three items consist of light brisk strokes to the right cheek and left cheek simultaneously, the right cheek and right hand simultaneously, and the left hand alone. Twenty such items are administered. If any errors are made, an additional trial of twenty items is performed.

Three types of errors are recorded; extinction errors when only one simultaneously applied stimulus is perceived, displacement errors when the patient indicates an area stimulated other than the face or hand, and adjunction errors when the patient indicates a stimulation in addition to those delivered. According to data collected on adults, three or more errors is indicative of cerebral dysfunction. Errors restricted to one side of the body are considered evidence of a lateralized sensory deficit. Errors on both sides are considered evidence of a bilateral sensory deficit or involvement of the mechanisms in brain or spinal cord mediating lateralized somatosensory functions (Centofanti & Smith, 1979).

The tests discussed above are merely representative of the types of measures available for the neuropsychological assessment of adolescents. None of these tests is sufficient by itself to reliably identify the presence or nature of organic impairment. However, when combined into a comprehensive battery and administered by a trained neuropsychologist, they can provide important information for the understanding of an individual adolescent's neuropsychological status.

Chapter 8

Personality Inventories and Behaviorally-Based Measures

The goal of administering personality inventories and behavioral checklists is to assess traits that are descriptive of a youth and to determine how these traits relate to the presenting problems. Psychologists have developed paper-and-pencil, self-report personality inventories and questionnaires, to be completed by parents or significant others, which may be either a list of true/false, yes/no questions, or rated on a continuum from "Not at all" to "Frequently." These instruments attempt to measure the cognitive, emotional, interpersonal, motivational, and additudinal characteristics of an individual.

Structured tests are objective in that an individual's pattern of responses is compared with that of specific reference groups. An attempt is made to provide normative data for these scales through empirical data collection. Scoring is generally conducted through hand-scoring keys or, in more recent times, by computer. Both types of scoring methods yield profiles which correspond to descriptions of personality.

Although there are hundreds of self-report scales that have been developed to assess personality, this chapter focuses on four that either have been used extensively in the assessment of adolescents, or are recent attempts to refine efforts in scale development directed specifically at adolescent populations. For adults, as well as for adolescents, the Minnesota Multiphasic Personality Inventory (MMPI) has been the most widely used and researched. However due to its length and other issues surrounding its relevance and interpretive value for adolescents, scales such as the Millon Adolescent Personality Inventory and Adolescent Multiphasic Personality Inventory have been created. By contrast, the Jesness Inventory was specifically developed as a multidimensional scale for assessing delinquent behavior in children and adolescents.

Another useful objective method for obtaining preliminary information is the use of behavior problem checklists and rating scales. These forms can be completed by teachers or by parents while the clinician is interviewing the adolescent. Once scored, this information will have screened for the incidence and severity of presenting problems as well as serve as a platform for further discussion with the family. Besides these screening functions, behavioral rating forms can be used to pinpoint target behaviors for intervention purposes, provide a way to monitor progress, and conduct evaluations for treatment effectiveness (Wilson & Prentice-Dunn, 1981). Through the use of such forms, the clinician can survey a vast number of behaviors in a timely fashion, then concentrate on specific behaviors through the successive stages of the assessment process.

Checklists and rating forms vary as to age range, breadth of problem areas covered, the specifity of the items, and settings for appropriate usage. They also differ in the number of items presented, from a low of 40 on the Adolescent Life Assessment Checklist (Gleser et al., 1977) to 600 on the Personality Inventory for Children (PIC) (Wirt et al., 1977). Most of these scales tend to cluster into two kinds of groupings, i.e. personality problems, such as anxiety and withdrawal, or conduct disorders (Evans and Nelson, 1977). Additional clusters — inadequacy–immaturity and subcultural delinquency — have also been identified (Quay, Morse, & Cutler, 1966; Quay, 1964).

The two measures chosen for review in this chapter, the Personality Inventory for Children (Wirt et al., 1977) and the Child Behavior Checklist and Child Behavior Profile (Achenbach & Edelbrock, 1978), offer clinicians the advantages of having both a standardized format for describing behaviors and a graphed profile of personality dimensions in a similar format to the MMPI. This twofold approach to the classification of childhood psychopathology provides practitioners and researchers with a unique opportunity to define personality factors within the context of behavior functioning.

THE MINNESOTA MULTIPHASIC
PERSONALITY INVENTORY
(MMPI)

Of all the objective personality instruments in psychology, the Minnesota Multiphasic Personality Inventory (MMPI) is the most widely used and most researched. Its construction began in the late 1930s by Starke Hathaway, Ph.D., and Jovian McKinley, M.D., from the University of Minnesota Hospitals, who recognized the need for an objective multidimensional instrument to assist in the identification of severe psychopathology. The originators of the test initially compiled a pool of more than 1000 items from various psychiatric textbooks, personality scales, and their own clinical experience and prepared them in a self-report true-false format. The eight clinical scales that emerged were named for the syndrome identified. These included: Hypochondriasis, Depression, Hysteria, Psychopathic Deviant, Paranoia, Psychasthenia, Schizophrenia, and Hypomania. Later, the Masculinity–Feminity and the Social Introversion scales were constructed and included as standard clinical scales. In response to criticisms of earlier personality inventories, the authors developed four validity indicators to detect deviant test-taking attitudes. The final version of 566 items was originally published in 1943 by the Psychological Corporation, and since 1982 University of Minnesota researchers have been involved in continuing efforts to increase validity and reliability studies of this measure.

There has also been considerable research in identifying critical sets of items within the MMPI to distinguish various problem areas of the respondents. The most promising of these "special" scales are: the 49-item MacAndrew (MAC) that attempts to identify substance abusers (MacAndrew, 1979); Welsh's 39-item Anxiety (A) and 40-item Repression (R) scales that reflect, respectively, feelings of distress and discomfort, and dimensions of excitability and aggressiveness (Welsh, 1956); and Barron's 68-item Ego Strength (Es) measure that attempts to predict the readiness for individual psychotherapy. Of these, the MAC scale has been most researched with adolescent populations and has shown promising utility for continued usage in this age group (Archer, 1987).

There has only recently been a renewed interest in the study of responses and norms for adolescent MMPI respondents. Most notable is the current restandarization project being completed at the University of Minnesota. This includes normative values for adolescents (15 to 18-year-olds) for the "special" scales based on Gottesman's followup analysis of the Minnesota statewide sample (cited and reproduced in Archer, 1987). The recognition that the stage of adolescence is marked by salient physiological and intellectual changes has led researchers to expect that individuals within this age group would interpret and respond to the MMPI questions in a different manner than adults. Empirical studies that delved into this issue have shown that this assumption is justified (Hathaway & Monachesi, 1963). The fact that adolescence is a transient developmental period where a high frequency of aberrant behaviors is likely to appear, supports the need for and use of distinct age norms in analyzing adolescent MMPI protocols (Archer, 1987).

There have been many findings that point to the tendency for adolescents to ascribe to severe symptomatologic features on the MMPI (e.g., Gottesman & Fishman, 1961). This is particularly true in items suggesting unusual experiences, higher incidences of impulsive actions, rebellious attitudes and social isolation (i.e., scales F, Pd, and Sc). For the adolescent the definition of normalcy may not be the same as for adults. In fact, without a set frame of reference for adolescent responses there would be a tendency to view their profiles as severely pathological. To readily interpret their responses based on adult norms would have an adverse effect on developing an accurate diagnostic impression as well as treatment intervention (Archer, 1984).

Unfortunately, many examiners still insist on using adult norms despite several convincing studies suggesting substantial age effects across population groupings. The fear of obscuring or overlooking significant clinical material is too strong. Even the earlier researchers would not go on record to suggest using only adolescent norms (Hathaway & Monachesi, 1963; Marks, Seeman, & Haller, 1974) although more recent reviews of the literature advocate the use of available tables for adolescent conversions and descriptions of personality (Greene, 1980; Williams, 1985). This lack of consensus among researchers and clinicians has produced considerable confusion in both assessment and treatment intervention for adolescents within the mental health system. According to Archer (1987), the most beneficial use of the MMPI when given to adolescents is to only convert the raw score values against adolescent norms, and not to utilize adult norms at all.

The MMPI can be administered to youngsters as young as 12 or 13 if their reading level is at least fifth to sixth grade (Dahlstrom, Welsh, & Dahlstrom, 1972, Williams, 1985). A quick screening can be done by an administration of the WRAT or by just allowing the youth to read the statements aloud. If reading is a problem, the examiner can either read the statements aloud to the adolescent (which can often quicken the administration time) or make the standardized audiotape , which can be ordered through National Computer Systems, available to the youngster.

Another overriding consideration in using the MMPI with adolescents is their immature ability in sustained attention, since the test can be an ordeal to a youngster who tends to be distractible. The card format of the MMPI, in which items are sorted into true or false stacks, is one way to hold the adolescent's attention more readily. Additionally, the use of an on-line computer for test administration may also serve better the needs of a reluctant respondent. And, of course, there needs to be a comfortable setting in which the adolescent can concentrate, in order to respond accurately to this lengthy test, and proper supervision to provide encouragement and structure. The clinician should be advised not to allow the adolescent to complete the inventory at home or on the residential unit, since privacy and confidentiality cannot be assured and the temptation to share the test with peers is great.

Another major problem that might beset the accurate administration and interpretation of the MMPI with younger respondents is their lack of emotional experience. Thus, an assessment of their developmental level is pertinent to decide whether the MMPI would be of relevance in the attainment of personality descriptions. The wording and meaning of many of the MMPI statements has always been problematic for adolescents. In fact, much of the current effort in revising and updating the MMPI has been directed towards making the instrument more relevant and consumable to adolescents.

In trying to overcome the lengthy process of administration, many abbreviated variations of the MMPI have been devised (Newmark & Thibodeau, 1979; Macbeth & Cadow, 1984). Butcher (1985) attempted to distinguish between these "short" forms, such as the 71-item "Mini-Mult" and the MMPI-168, and the more generally accepted abbreviated version, which simply consists of the administration of the first 399 items on Form R. His main thesis was that while the latter version could produce all basic validity and clinical scales (although not the special scales), the use of the "short" forms could not produce reliable profiles and that these forms have not been sufficiently validated against external criteria. Researchers have shown that there tends to be over a 50 per cent difference in codetypes when comparisons are made between standard administrations and these "short" forms (Lueger, 1983; Hoffman & Butcher, 1975).

Thus, the use of shorter versions of the MMPI is plagued with many problems (Archer, 1987). Since there are already difficulties in the interpretation of adolescent profiles, the introduction of another questionable procedure makes the attained results even more equivocal. Further, although attempts to tailor the MMPI for adolescent respondents may save time and energy, the results are likely to be inaccurate and cause much inconsistency in attempting to integrate the profile with the rest of the available testing data. The best suggestion is to attempt the initial 399 items and, if time allows or special questions persist, try to administer all 566 items.

Because of the aforementioned problem areas in the administration of the MMPI to adolescents, the key to interpretation is being flexibile. Besides the use of established adolescent norms, the examiner should consult the available codetype personality information that describes adolescent behavior (e.g., Marks et al., 1974) and integrate this information with clinical correlates from adult populations (e.g., Graham, 1977; Greene, 1980). In addition, a much less rigid approach to interpreting the validity scales for adolescent profiles is warranted. This is especially relevant for scale F, which seems to have very different implications for adolescents than for adult populations (Archer, 1987). For example, adolescents have been shown to endorse a higher frequency of scale F items than adults, and will endorse a number of critical items due to their tendency to exaggerate their symptomology and to complete the inventory quickly or carelessly. Also, studies have shown correlations between high F respondents and delinquent behavior (e.g., Kanun & Monachesi, 1960). To eliminate an adolescent profile due to a high F value would seem counterproductive to a clinician whose job is to seek clues regarding individual behavior.

Because of the current trend in updating the MMPI and the increased reliance on computer administration and interpretation, the MMPI will most likely undergo a great transformation, especially in regard to applying its use to adolescent populations. However, caution should be used until these newer norms and interpretive strategies are researched. For now, the MMPI should be used as a rough guide to describing individual psychopathology rather than as a diagnostic tool. This is especially true concerning adolescents, whose responses may be a reflection of normal adolescent turmoil. Thus, particular attention needs to be directed towards limiting descriptive statements about the adolescent as reflecting long-standing characteristics, and certain reservations should be used in making broad descriptive statements about the adolescent client without confirmation from other available test information.

THE MILLON ADOLESCENT PERSONALITY INVENTORY (MAPI)

The Millon Adolescent Personality Inventory (MAPI) was developed by Millon, Green, and Meagher (1977, 1982) to address the specific considerations of assessing adolescents through the use of a paper-and-pencil inventory. The creation of the MAPI was based on the dissatisfaction with the theoretical limitations of interpreting adolescent personality from scales devised and normed for either primarily adult (e.g., Minnesota Multiphasic Inventory) or child (e.g., Personality Inventory for Children) populations. Toward this end, the creators of the MAPI contend that "the questions of which the inventory is composed are presented in a language that teenagers use and deal with matters they understand and find relevant to their concerns and experiences" (Millon, Green, & Meagher, 1982, p. 1). By limiting both the development and empirical validation of the MAPI to adolescents (13–18-year age range), Millon et al. (1982) sought to more clearly identify personality styles, concerns, and behaviors prevalent with youngsters of this specific developmental age.

In introducing their scale, these researchers delineated the numerous advantages of utilizing an inventory targeted toward adolescents. Specifically, the administration of the MAPI is tailored to meet the needs of adolescents by making the inventory both brief in nature (i.e., the MAPI consists of 150 true-false questions, with most adolescents completing the instrument in under 20, minutes) and in constructing the reading requirements to be on a sixth grade level (Millon et al., 1982). Additional advantages of the MAPI include: (a) it was based on both adolescent developmental theory (Erikson, 1968; Offer, 1969) and on Millon's own personality theory;

(b) specific test items were constructed with the assistance of school guidance counselors and psychologists, working directly with normal and abnormal adolescent populations; (c) the test is based on assessing both underlying personality traits and problem behaviors, as well as the adolescent's own expressed concerns; (d) it is used in school settings by counselors interested in assisting the adolescents with a more successful school adjustment and in clinical settings by psychologists in order to uncover personality attributes and problem areas so as to plan cogent treatment programs; and (e) it was developed through generally sound psychometric and statistical procedures (Brown, 1985; Millon et al., 1982). Finally, the interpreted adolescent MAPI protocol not only delineates the adolescent's current personality functioning but also stipulates recommendations for treatment planning, thereby directly linking personality assessment with intervention strategies.

The MAPI is divided into three different sections, labeled Personality Styles, Expressed Concerns, and Behavioral Correlates, with each section consisting of a number of specific scales. The Personality Styles section contains eight scales (Introversion, Inhibited, Cooperative, Sociable, Confident, Forceful, Respectful, Sensitive) which are based on Millon's (1969, 1981) theory of personality development and functioning. Specifically, Millon, (1981), in presenting his "biosocial learning theory," asserted that adult pathological personality functioning can be conceptualized along three dimensions: (a) the *active–passive dimension*, which entails the degree to which the individual "takes the initiative in shaping surrounding events or whether behavior is largely reactive to those events," (b) the *pleasure–pain dimension*, which stipulates that behaviors are directed either toward "events which are attractive or positively reinforcing" or "away from those which are aversive or negatively reinforcing," and (c) *the self–other dimension*, which details that the source of reinforcement is either the self or others (p. 58). From these three polarities, Millon (1981) postulated "11 different personality patterns" illustrative of abnormal and maladjusted coping strategies (p. 60). The Personality Style items on the MAPI reflect Millon et al.'s (1981) interpretation of the manner in which variants of these adult styles are represented in adolescents. Therefore assessment of the degree to which the adolescent is active or passive, oriented toward or away from others, and toward rewarding or punishing experiences is reflected in the scales which constitute the Personality Styles section (Brown, 1985). High scores on individual scales indicate more "habitual and maladaptive" modes of functioning in the areas of "thinking, relating and feeling" (Millon et al., 1982, p. 32). Individual personality configurations are established by synthesizing the highest two or three scales.

The Expressed Concerns section is also comprised of eight scales (Self Concept, Body Comfort, Sexual Acceptance, Peer Security, Social Tolerance, Family Rapport, and Academic Acceptance). These scales reflect "feelings and attitudes the adolescent may experience about issues that tend to concern most youngsters at one time or another" (Millon et al., 1981, p. 4). Specifically, items of Expressed Concerns ask adolescents to make assessments of their own functioning with regard to numerous age-related developmental tasks. The adolescent's own perceptions of their relative success or failure on these tasks is compared with a "cross section of teenagers of the same sex and age" (Millon et al., 1982). Elevations above 85 within a scale area indicate that the adolescent is admitting to feeling very concerned about the particular developmental task (Millon et al., 1982).

The third section, Behavioral Correlates, is comprised of four scales (Impulse Control, Societal Conformity, Scholastic Achievement, and Attendance Consistency). They measure the "extent to which the responses" of the adolescent "are similar to those who have been identified by counselors and clinicians as evidencing troublesome behaviors such as impulsivity, social noncompliance, underachievement and nonattendance" (Millon et al., 1982, p. 33). Individual scale elevations above 75 indicate a high degree of admitted similarity between the adolescent's behaviors and that of those youngsters already identified as demonstrating scale-specific aberrant behaviors.

Additionally, the MAPI includes three validity scores (Adjustment Score, Reliability Index, and Validity Index), which are used to evaluate the veracity of the completed protocols. The adjustment score entails modifying the scores on the Expressed Concern scales based on attained scores on the Personality Style scales. The purpose of the adjustment scores is to "build in a correction for psychological defensiveness and complaint tendencies" (Millon et al., 1982, p. 17). The second validity measure, the Reliability Index, consists of three questions asking the adolescent to indicate the degree to which they agree that endorsed items reflect enduring traits and to the degree of seriousness with which they regard the testing situation. Obtaining a score of 1 or above casts the reliability of the protocol into question (Millon et al., 1982). The Validity Index, which reflects the level of attentiveness and seriousness the adolescent possesses in completing the inventory, measures the presence of random responding, with an index above 1 suggesting a questionable protocol. Finally, the MAPI also identifies critical items endorsed by the adolescent which "suggest specific problem areas" for further exploration (Millon et al., 1982, p. 34).

Scoring and interpretation of the MAPI is computer-automated. Clinicians utilizing the MAPI must mail in, teleprocess, or obtain microcomputer software from National Computer Systems in order to receive an interpreted protocol. Scored protocols include a profile of raw and base rate scores for all scales. Base rate scores, instead of standard scores, are used in the MAPI due to violation of the assumption of a "normal" distribution for "the traits or dimensions being measured" (Millon et al., 1982, p. 15). A computer-generated narrative of four or five pages follows the profile and outlines each section. Additionally, a list of endorsed critical items is provided. Finally the report ends with a short narrative on treatment implications. Two forms of the interpretive report are available. One aids the clinician by making some suggestions for diagnosis and therapy strategies, and one helps school counselors by framing the interpretive summary more in line with concerns of school personnel (Millon et al., 1982).

There are a number of concerns about the validity of the MAPI (Brown, 1985; Widiger, 1985). Some of the most critical issues are: (a) the lack of published validation research on the inventory other than the test manual, (b) questions regarding the validation measures used (Widiger, 1985), (c) the high degree of overlap in the items used for a variety of scales (Widiger, 1985), and (d) the sole reliance on computer-generated interpretation of protocols (Brown, 1985). Additionally, the MAPI is subject to the general question of whether adolescent personality is stable to the point that information gathered through such an inventory can actually be legitimately used by a clinician to make statements regarding underlying and habitual coping styles. With regard to the MAPI itself, some questions can be raised as to the wisdom of Millon et al. (1982) in adapting his theory of adult pathology to an adolescent population. While the promise of the MAPI has not been totally realized, it represents an important step in the development of assessment instruments targeted to specific populations. The potential value of the MAPI lies in more clearly identifying adolescent personality functioning. However, further research and modification will be needed before the potential importance of this assessment instrument can be actualized.

THE ADOLESCENT MULTIPHASIC PERSONALITY INVENTORY (AMPI)

In attempting to rectify the weaknesses in using the MMPI with adolescents, Bruce Duthie, a leading researcher of the MMPI, has created a similarly structured objective scale for the clinical evaluation of adolescents — the Adolescent Multiphasic Personality Inventory (AMPI) (Duthie, 1985). The development of this instrument is based on the assumption that the MMPI is too long, too sophisticated, and has too high a reading level and too many scoring procedures for effective use with adolescents.

In order to ameliorate these deficiencies, Duthie has devised a scale that offers a single procedure for scoring, lowers the reading level to grade four, provides scoring keys and the opportunity for on-site computerized scoring and interpretation, and reduces the number of test items to 133, structured along the lines of the MMPI scales. Also in concordance with the MMPI, Duthie has added three validity scales to assess test-taking strategies. The

AA—G

only exception to this similarity is Scale 5, called the FEM scale on the AMPI. This particular scale is a general measure of femininity. A person scoring high on this scale is viewed as endorsing feminine cultural interest patterns. This scale is not reversed as on the MMPI. Correlations between the AMPI and parallel MMPI scales are between .38 for the LIE-L scales and .69 for the PAS-Pt scales. Most of these comparative correlations fall within the high .50s and low .60s range, indicating a moderate correspondence.

Scoring the AMPI is relatively easy, as the author provides two scoring keys (i.e., sticks) in order to total the true and false responses. After tallying these marks for each scale, the examiner places the number in the specified raw score box on either the male or female adolescent profiles. The raw scores are then plotted on the respective graph with dots and the dots are then connected.

Duthie describes three strategies for interpreting the AMPI. The first is configural interpretation based on factor analytic studies, rather than a multi-point coding based on MMPI interpretation, since like MMPI short forms, this has not shown to be effective and is likely to draw false inferences about the adolescent. The second level of interpretation is based on viewing the individual scales independently of one another, while the third level is based on individual item interpretation.

Through his early work with the scale, Duthie has found four factors that comprise the AMPI. These include the neurotic factor (scales DEP, HYS, and FEM), a conduct disorder factor (scales PPD and MAN), a validity factor (scales LIE and KOR), and a psychotic factor (scales PAR, PAS, SCZ, and SIN). A factor is usually interpreted if the average T score of the scales composing the factor is 65 or greater. For example, if an adolescent obtains an average T score of 65 or more on the neurotic cluster of scales, it is likely that he or she is depressed, emotionally labile, and interpersonally sensitive. This scale cluster may also be elevated when the adolescent is going through a period of acute stress. Those adolescents who score high on Factor 2 (conduct disorder) are acknowledging involvement in delinquent activities and expressing adjustment problems to societal constraints. Besides tending to be impulsive, hedonistic, and selfish, they are also viewed as having poor peer relations and being manipulative. High scores on the third factor (validity) suggest that the adolescent was attempting to place him or herself in a favorable position, while lower scores combined with moderate elevation on the other scales usually indicate adaptive functioning. The fourth factor (indicative of psychosis) represents those adolescents who are acknowledging psychotic symptoms. Scoring high on this cluster of scales is often associated with adolescents who are likely to be alienated, socially incompetent, suspicious, and at times may display grossly bizarre behavior.

To aid in individual item interpretation, Duthie has grouped item clusters into nine categories. These include: physical symptoms (e.g., "I throw up often"); psychotic symptoms (e.g., "I have strange and different thoughts"); depressive symptoms (e.g., "I lack confidence in myself"); anxiety symptoms (e.g., "I have trouble keeping my mind on one thing"); hostile impulses (e.g., "At times I feel like breaking things"); antisocial behavior (e.g., "I have hurt animals"); sexual concerns ("Sexual matters worry me"); alienation and paranoia (e.g., "Someone is out to get me"); and hypomania (e.g., "I have done dangerous things for the thrill of it"). As can be seen from this group of items, the AMPI was directly derived from the MMPI. However, Duthie eliminated those items with a high social desirability rating found by the authors of the MMPI (Dahlstrom, Welsh, and Dahlstrom, 1972). Other items that were removed included those that had a test–retest correlation of less than .80 and those that contained complicated sentence structure. The remaining items were all reworded and nine items were added to the K(OR) scale, since many had been eliminated after the removal of complex sentences.

Duthie himself acknowledges several weaknesses in the use of this scale. These include (a) the absence of special scales such as those found on the MMPI; (b) the fact that the scales were not developed to specifically reflect adolescent concerns; and (c) the downward extension not being lower than the fourth grade. In addition, since the normative population was relatively small (a total of 320 adolescents in two studies) and predominantly white and non-Hispanic, precaution must be used in judging its accuracy for a broader population. Concurrent validity studies correlating the AMPI with the MMPI, the SCL-90-R (Derogatis, 1977), and the Diagnostic Inventory of Personality and Symptoms (Vincent, 1984) provide the framework for interpreting the individual AMPI scales. These studies indicate that the AMPI is similar to its parent test (i.e., the MMPI). Thus, the test holds much promise for assessing adolescents, due to its brevity and lower reading comprehension level, but much more research and actual clinical impressions regarding its usefulness are needed, and fuller use will have to await the passing of time.

THE JESNESS INVENTORY

The Jesness Inventory, developed by Carl F. Jesness in the early 1960s, was constructed to aid in the personality assessment of emotionally disturbed children and adolescents, especially those with delinquent backgrounds. It is a 155-item true–false questionnaire that yields scores on eleven empirically derived scales. The development of the instrument was an attempt to produce a structured scale that would respond to changes in attitude, could be used with children as young as eight, would be multidimensional in scope, and could predict delinquent problems within a single measure (Jesness, 1983).

The Jesness Inventory Manual contains 35 pages of helpful and practical tips on how to use the test (Keyser & Sweetland, 1984). For a more in-depth approach to understanding the development of the test, one can refer to the original articles stemming from the five-year research and treatment program where the scales were first used (Jesness, 1962; 1963). Besides the manual, which contains norms for males and females ages 8–18, other materials required for its use are the scoring stencils and profile sheets that can be obtained from the publisher (Consulting Psychologists Press). A computer-scoring service has been developed over the years that also offers a classification system of nine personality subtypes. Considerable effort is going into research on this system. Details can be found in *Classifying Offenders: The Jesness Inventory Classification System Technical Manual* (Jesness & Wedge, 1983).

Like the MMPI, the raw scale scores of the Jesness have to be converted into T scores, with the mean being 50 and a standard deviation of 10. Scores below 30 and above 70 are viewed as interpretable, once the profile has been plotted. Although no validity scales were specifically incorporated into the instrument, one must be suspicious of the results if the Asocial Index, Repression, and Denial are greater than 60, if one of these subscales is higher than 65, or if an adolescent who is already known as being delinquent scores low on all the subscales (Keyser & Sweetland, 1984).

In reviewing the profile, the clinician can examine four of the scales that reflect the degree of "treatability". These include Asocial Index, Withdrawal, Immaturity, and Social Anxiety. For instance, a score high on Immaturity, which is a reflection of impulsivity, and high on Repression is usually indicative of lower intellectual functioning. This, in turn, would contraindicate a recommendation for verbal, insight-oriented therapeutic approaches, and, conversely, may indicate that behavioral and/or supportive therapies may be most helpful. In contrast, high scores on Withdrawal and/or Social Anxiety seem to suggest that an adolescent is motivated for an insight-oriented therapeutic intervention as he or she is acknowledging an uncomfortable present situation. As one would expect, a high score on the Asocial Index (>75) is a poor prognosticator for treatment effectiveness.

Since much of the profile interpretation is based on clinical judgment, users should be aware that they are only generating hypotheses concerning a particular youth's personality and need much corroboration from supporting sources before making definitive statements. However, there are a number of specific profile types that provide an interesting classification of delinquent behavior. For example, a delinquent who is considered sociopathic is likely to have a low score on Social Anxiety (nothing to inhibit behavior), a high score on Alienation (blames adults for problems), a high score on Autism (a selfish outlook with a falsely inflated sense of self-esteem), and a low score on Immaturity ("cooler" than peers). A delinquent who tends to be aggressive and antisocial would likely have high scores on Value Orientation (external),

Immaturity (impulsive), Autism (poor judgment and distorted reality), Alienation, Manifest Anger, and a low score on Denial (i.e, minimal ego functioning). The "inadequate" type of delinquent is profiled as having high scores on Autism (little thinking) and Repression (no insight), moderately high scores on Withdrawal and Social Anxiety (likes to be among delinquent types but often gets beaten up) and the Asocial Index (not a hard core type), and low scores on Alienation (prefers others to be in authority and a self-blamer) and Manifest Anger (no intensity). This type of youth is likely to be socially awkward, impulsive and have a low self-regard. This is the kind of child that usually acts out to seek attention and follows the lead of others without thinking about the possible consequences.

A recent critique of the inventory indicated that several of the scales — i.e., Social Maladjustment, Value Orientation, and the Asocial index — did indeed meet the original objectives of the author, as they seem to uncover delinquent attitudes and degree of delinquent activity (Keyser & Sweetland, 1984). When used as a means to obtain antisocial attitudes and behavior, the instrument has been quite successful. If the examiner needs an actuarial base for placement and decisionmaking or wants additional insight into delinquent attitudes, involvement, and associated personality characteristics, the Jesness Inventory seems to be a preferred test.

The Jesness Inventory seems to be deficient when it is given to a broad population of children, since it is so heavily weighted toward delinquency. Thus, clinicians should be cautious in their interpretations of this personality inventory. Another major weakness of the Jesness is its absence of items concerning sexuality. This is mainly due to the initial investigation, which was based on interviewing 8 to 14-year-old males. As with many instruments that have been normed on a specific reference group, the best way to utilize the Jesness is as an adjunct to history, homelife, and peer environment, and within the context of a larger battery of personality tests.

THE PERSONALITY INVENTORY
FOR CHILDREN (PIC)

The Personality Inventory for Children was constructed as an objective multidimensional measure of behavior, affect, ability, and family functioning in children and adolescents from age six to 16 years (Wirt, Lachar, Klinedinst, & Seat, 1977). This true–false inventory, containing 600 items, is usually completed by the parent or long-term guardian. Its main purpose is to provide screening information for the examiner before a formal psychological evaluation, in order to concentrate on specific problem areas. The brief statements focus attention on both the child and his or her family relationships (e.g., "My child has been difficult to manage"). The person answering the questionnaire is provided with an administration booklet and an answer sheet. The form is scored in a fashion similar to that of the MMPI, with templates and raw scores converted into T-scores. On-line computer administration is also available, with various interpretive options based on the number of completed questions (Lachar, 1987). Three validity scales are graphed, along with 12 clinical scales and an overall Adjustment Scale.

The standardization sample included 2390 children, approximately equally distributed by sex and number throughout the age range. The validity scales that were added to the inventory include: a Lie Scale (L) that, when elevated, is indicative of a defensive style of responding relating to denying child and family problems; an F Scale that addresses the intensity of symptoms; and a Defensiveness (DEF) Scale that shows that the informant is responding in a consistent pattern of either denying aberrant behaviors and conflicts or placing the blame for the problems on external sources.

The 12 clinical scales measure an assortment of cognitive and emotional areas. The scales related to intelligence and academics include: Achievement (ACH) (addressing academic problems, distractibility, impulsiveness, and poor motivation); Poor Readers (PIAT); Intellectual Screening (IS) (differentiating normals from retarded); and the Development Scale (DVL) Scale, a broad-based measure correlating with both cognitive and emotional growth. Emotional concerns are reflected by a Somatic Concern Scale (SOM) that addresses physical ailments and their frequency and severity; an Internalization (INT) Scale, collapsed from statements relating to withdrawal, depression, and anxiety; a Depression Scale (D) that includes symptoms such as crying, loss of interest, pessimism, and moodiness; a Withdrawal Scale (WDL), indicative of a lack of emotional warmth combined with physical and social isolation; an Anxiety Scale (ANX) measuring the degree of worry and irrational fears; and a Social Skills Scale (SSK) that identifies the lonely child and some of the reasons for having few friends.

A Psychosis Scale (PSY) was developed to differentiate normal children from those suffering from various kinds of psychosis, and has only minimal overlap with the other scales. Children that have been diagnosed as psychotic usually obtain scores over 100T (Lachar & Gdowski, 1979). A scale was also created to identify those children seen as emotionally labile, restless, impulsive, and as having disturbed interpersonal relations. T-scores in the low 60s on this Hyperactive Scale (HPR) have been found to correctly identify this population most of the time. A Delinquency Scale (DLQ) describes those youth that are somewhat antisocial and have problems with following generally accepted guideline and societal restraints. Finally, statements that relate to family cohesion and effectiveness are subsumed under the Family Scale (FAM). These items, which also offer little overlap with the other scales, view those statements concerning family life that reflect harmony and communication. Besides the 12 basic clinical scales, 17 supplemental scales have been derived which address specific aspects of functioning, such as adolescent maladjustment, aggression, and ego strength.

The PIC, like most behaviorally-oriented measures, is relatively easy to administer. In addition, efforts were made to demonstrate sound psychometric properties. For example, test–retest reliability demonstrated coefficients of .71 and higher for intervals up to 102 days. Validity studies have shown a congruency between adolescent PIC and MMPI respondents (Lachar, Butkus, & Hryhorczuk, 1978) as well as the accurate prediction of which hyperactive children will respond to medication (Voelker, 1979). Also, in the development of the scale, efforts were made to collect a large normative sample that was representative of census data at every age level.

However, there are also limitations to the PIC of which an examiner should be aware before making interpretations. The person completing the questionnaire should be someone who has been with the youth since early childhood. This eliminates its use with almost everyone besides the child's parents or long-term guardians. Another caution relating to interpretation of the scales concerns the transformation of raw scores into T-values. Each T-value needs to be interpreted against the criterion group that has been researched. The aforementioned differences in T-values for interpretation of psychotic children ($T \geq 100$) versus hyperactive children ($T \geq 62$) is one such example. Thus, there is a larger variation in interpretation of T-scores on the PIC than the MMPI (Goldman, Stein, & Guerry, 1983).

Although there are some limitations to the PIC and questions concerning the assumptions on which it was based, it has been effective when used as a preliminary screening device to confirm initial impressions, in addition to discovering problem areas that may have been overlooked during the interviewing process. It has also been found to aid in establishing a diagnosis. The validity scales seem also to be useful in detecting biases that are not usually included in other behavioral inventories. With the advent of computerized assessment, a considerable data base of PIC responses has been collected. (Lachar, 1987). This has, for example, allowed the establishment of two and three scale point actuarial interpretations, in a similar manner as with the MMPI. With the additional development of computer usage of the PIC, its clinical utility will be greatly enhanced.

THE CHILD BEHAVIOR CHECKLIST

The Child Behavior Checklist, along with Revised Child Behavior Profile, is the culmination of many years of research by Thomas Achenbach and his colleague Craig Edelbrock (Achenbach, 1966; Achenbach & Edelbrock, 1983; Achenbach & Edelbrock; 1978). Divided into two parts, the scale assesses a youth's social competencies and behavioral difficulties. The social competence scale is composed of 20 items, which address functioning in the areas of interpersonal relations, extracurricular activities, and overall academic performance. Problems in behavior are indicated by a checklist of 113 brief descriptive statements rated on a three-point continuum, from not true to frequent occurrences. The scale, which takes approximately 20 minutes to complete, is completed by the parent or guardian and instructs the respondent to concentrate on those actions and symptoms occurring during the previous six months.

With the information derived from the questionnaire, a profile can be plotted based on two "broad band" factors (Internalizing and Externalizing) and nine "narrow band" factors. There are five "narrow band" scales included within the Internalizing section. These include: Schizoid or Anxious, Depressed, Uncommunicative, Obsessive-Compulsive, Somatic Complaints, and Social Withdrawal. The scales that constitute the Externalizing part of the scale include: Hyperactive, Aggressive and Delinquent.

Separate norms have been extensively researched for three age groupings — 4–5, 6–11, and 12–16 years. Standard scores have been derived for both the broad and narrow band factors with a mean of 50 and standard deviation of 10. The behavior profile represents a clear graphic picture of a particular youth's behavioral functioning in regard to the normative sample for that sex and age grouping. Manual scoring with templates in order to plot the profile takes approximately 45 minutes. Achenbach currently has a computer software package that will score the form and print a graphic profile of the factor scores in much less time.

In attempting to enhance its clinical utility, Achenbach and Edelbrock have developed several ancillary scales to supplement the information gathered from the parent reports (Achenbach & Edelbrock, 1983). They have created a Teachers' Report Form which extends the information gathering process to include educational background, adaptive skills related to the classroom, and classroom-specific behavior management problems. The checklist portion of the scale has also been modified for relevance to the classroom experience. The authors have also created adaptations of the scale in the form of a direct observation instrument which allows an experienced observer to describe a youth's functioning in several classroom situations and rate the behaviors on a 96-item checklist. Another supplement to the reporting by the parents is the Youth Self-Report. This checklist is designed to be used by adolescents from age 11 to 18 and is present in the first person. The research stemming from the reliability and validity of these supplemental scales is somewhat limited at this time but there seems to be much clinical usefulness in their continued use.

Like other behavior rating forms, the Child Behavior Checklist is subject to problems relating to responder bias due to either inaccuracies or distortions by the persons completing the form. In addition, the pioneering research primarily used outpatients and may thus underestimate behavior characteristics of inpatient populations. However, the scale is convenient to administer, and with the use of a computer, easily scored and graphed. As more data become avaliable to researchers and clinicians, the instrument will begin to be used with much more assurance.

Chapter 9

Projective Techniques

The use of projective techniques offers adolescents a broader range of responses than yes/no questionnaires or tests of intelligence and achievement. The major assumption behind their usage is that an individual will project portions of his/her personality or response style when presented with a sufficiently ambiguous stimulus. That is, when individuals are confronted with a certain stimulus or situation they respond in their own unique manner. Thus, the trained clinician can infer an adolescent's various needs, concerns, coping abilities, perceptions, and reality testing based on the quantity and quality of his/her responses to such stimuli as inkblots, drawings, cards with pictured themes, and incomplete sentences.

Projective testing may be particularly useful in determining severe psychopathology, including thought and affective disorder, and in helping determine suicidal risk or other potential problems of impulse control. Clinicians can also provide a more complete determination of adequacy of defenses and the intensity of different affects, and be able to discover underlying fears or disturbing thoughts. For those adolescents who may be defensive or hostile toward structured tests, the use of unstructured tests may also offer an outlet for a safe expression of anger or other threatening emotions.

Although projective techniques vary extensively, this chapter will focus on the most widely used projective tests and scoring systems. These include: the Rorschach Inkblot Test, with emphasis on the Exner scoring system; various drawing directives, including the Draw-A-Person, Draw-A-Person-In-The-Rain, and Family Drawings; the Thematic Apperception Test (TAT); and incomplete sentence blanks. These tests are generally used in varying combinations within a test battery to provide corroborating evidence about an individual's emotional functioning.

THE RORSCHACH TEST

The Rorschach is one of the most widely used projective techniques. In fact, it has consistently served as the cornerstone evaluative instrument in making an assessment of the emotional life and personality characteristics of the referred client. The Rorschach has great clinical value and utility in terms of mining the richness of adolescent personality functioning. However, the clinician must exercise extreme care in the use and interpretation of Rorschach protocols such that an adequate assessment of the adolescent is achieved. The Rorschach is quite clearly a very controversial evaluative device. The debate encompasses those who would agree that the Rorschach is often "no more than free associating to the patient's free associations" as well as those clinicians who believe strongly that an individual's inner life is accurately projected onto the Rorschach cards, while others maintain a position in between (Beck, 1981, p. 41). The clinician interested in using the Rorschach as part of an assessment battery must be knowledgeable about the development, administration, and limits of interpretation of this particular technique, in order to assure the accuracy and validity of its use. In specifically utilizing the Rorschach with an adolescent population, the clinician must also be very familiar with adolescent development, and how it differs from both normal and deviant performance of children and adults on the Rorschach.

The Rorschach consists of ten separate cards, each of which contain a single, completely bilaterally symmetrical inkblot. Five of the cards consist only of black, white and grey hues, while an additional two inkblots also contain variants of red color. The remaining three inkblots contain an array of colors. Exner (1986) reports that Hermann Rorschach's original development and experimentation with the cards was done with the belief of ultimately originating a perceptual task which could "lend itself to a sophisticated diagnostic approach for the differentiation of schizophrenia" (Exner, 1986, p. 3). Unfortunately, Rorschach died before he was able to complete his work, and in part the great divergence in the use and interpretation of the Rorschach can be attributed to the fact that others have had to speculate on Hermann Rorschach's actual intentions. While most clinicians and researchers who have been involved with the use of the Rorschach can basically agree that it is a "perceptual–cognitive task" (Weiner, 1986, p. 143), there is great controversy as to the degree to which the subjects' offered cognitions can be interpreted in terms of the degree of perceptual accuracy and content presented.

Exner (1986) points out that the generation of Rorschach researchers after Hermann Rorschach's death largely deviated from his strict empirical investigation of the stimulus cards. With the dissemination of Freudian theory, use of the Rorschach changed, from a solely perceptual–organizational task to concentration and investigation of the content areas offered by subjects (Exner, 1986). Within this context, the Rorschach was viewed as an ambiguous instrument which allowed for the individual's "unconscious psychic material" to be projected onto the cards and then verbalized to the examiner (Sundberg, 1977, p. 203). According to the projective hypothesis, these verbalizations were not random but instead revealed the inner psychological processes of the individual. Consequently, by interpreting Rorschach responses, assumptions concerning the underlying personality dynamics could be drawn. The five dominant Rorschach scoring systems (Klopfer, Beck, Piotrowski, Hertz, and Rapaport-Schafer), which developed after Hermann Rorschach's death, varied widely in their adherence to a more empirical conceptualization and were more psychodynamic in their approach to administration, scoring, and interpretation (Exner, 1986). In consideration of assessment of adolescents, it is very interesting to note that as a group these five systems devoted very little attention to empirical investigations with adolescent subjects in comparison with the energy spent assessing and interpreting adult and child protocols.

In an effort to return to Hermann Rorschach's intended original, empirical use of his stimulus cards as a perceptual-cognitive task, while disavowing the use of the Rorschach as a sort of "X-Ray of the mind" (Exner, 1986, p. 24), Exner (1974, 1986) developed a sixth Rorschach system encompassing standards for administration, scoring, and interpretation. The Comprehensive System emerged from a massive review of the published literature (both from research investigations and clinical papers), an initial study of more than 800 Rorschach protocols, and comparisons between the five existing Rorschach systems (Exner, 1986). In creating the Comprehensive System, Exner (1974, 1986) was primarily interested in originating a system with a scoring procedure that produced a high degree of interrater reliability. In other words, two clinicians with the same battery would be able to achieve a high rate of agreement as to their scoring of the protocol. In establishing such a scoring system, Exner's (1974, 1986) goal was to increase the science of Rorschach scoring and interpretation while decreasing the dependence on clinical lore. In addition, once a data bank of patient and nonpatient records of persons from age 5 to adulthood had been amassed, not only could a client's individual record be compared with a normative sample, but interpretation of Rorschach responses would be judged against the individual's same age peers (Weiner, 1986). Therefore, the implications of the Comprehensive System are quite impressive, as interpretation of adolescent protocols no longer need to rely on individual clinicians trying to adapt child or adult Rorschach research and clinical theories to adolescent populations.

Exner's (1985) guidelines for examination are quite clear and the interested reader should consult Exner (1986) and Exner and Weiner (1982). The examiner is to position him- or herself alongside the client, therefore avoiding a face-to-face arrangement (Exner, 1986). Exner maintains that this seating arrangement is less threatening to the client, and also allows the examiner to more clearly identify the client's use of the blot areas. Prior to actual administration of the Rorschach, Exner also recommends some introduction of the task to the client. This is especially important when examining adolescent populations, as some structuring of the task usually decreases anxiety and resistance. In testing adolescents, a straightforward approach is highly recommended. Therefore a good introduction to the task would be: "We are now going to do the inkblot test. Have you ever heard of it?" (Exner, 1985, p. 2). If the adolescent responds that she or he is not familiar with the test, then Exner et al. (1985) stipulates that the following further introductions be made: "It's just a series of inkblots that I'll show you and I want you to tell me what they look like to you" (p. 2). If the adolescent admits to some familiarity with the Rorschach it is important for the examiner to gain information on how long ago the youngster was tested, in what setting, and why the testing was done (Exner et al., 1985).

Adolescent clients often question the rationale of the test prior to administration. In these circumstances, Exner (1985) advocates an open approach; for example, "it is a test that gives us some information about your personality and by having that information we can . . . " (p. 2). In circumstances where the adolescent is suspicious or guarded, an examiner can quite simply offer that "it is a test that gives some idea of how you think." In order to gain a meaningful Rorschach protocol, it is important that the adolescent feel comfortable in starting the Rorschach; however, the examiner must be careful not to answer questions which would influence the adolescent's responses to the cards. Any questions by the adolescent which seem to compromise the administration of the Rorschach should be answered after completion of the test.

In administering the Rorschach to adolescents, it is important that the examiner remain sensitive to the specific issues often presented by adolescent clients. Adolescents as a rule are generally very self-conscious about their performance and many youngsters can be intimidated by the task, fearing the examiner will have "X-ray vision" into their minds. Other adolescents may present as guarded and hostile. These clients often are angry about being evaluated and can become quite oppositional in their reaction to the Rorschach. It is not infrequent for either type of youngster to be presented with Card I and for them to respond "it is an inkblot" or "I don't see anything." It is important at this point for the examiner to remain neutral and not to take either a defensive or authoritarian position, as this will be threatening to the anxious client and could result in a power struggle with the defiant and oppositional youngster. Instead, the examiner should simply respond "take your time, everyone can find something . . . just tell me what you see" (Exner, 1986, p. 67–68). Very few youngsters after this prompt continue to resist involvement in the task. For those extreme cases a decision should be made by the examiner as to the utility in pursuing the testing session, since there is little likelihood that an adolescent so resistive to the process can produce a Rorschach record that will yield enough information for a valid interpretation.

Adolescent clients can also be resistant in the inquiry phase of the Rorschach administration. It takes a clinician skilled in working with adolescents as well as with Exner's inquiry protocol to be able to gain Rorschach data that is scorable and valid. Frequently, oppositional and defiant adolescents lose patience with the repetitive nature of the inquiry process. This often occurs as either a product of the adolescent's frustration and anger or that of the examiner. Specifically, some very guarded young-sters may interpret the examiner's questioning during the inquiry phase as an indication that they have given the wrong answer. Even the most innocuous statements, such as "I'm not sure I see it as you do," can be threatening for the youngster who is sensitive to rejection. In these circumstances, it is impera-tive that the examiner remain neutral and avoid any possible statements which could be interpreted as judgemental. Furthermore, it is also essential that the examiner memorize the variety of statements allowed by the Exner protocol during the inquiry phase, so that the adolescent isn't repeatedly being asked the exact same question.

Adolescents often become resistant during the inquiry process when they perceive that the examiner is frustrated. This often occurs in brief records where the adolescent is witholding and the examiner is struggling to ascertain the necessary information in order to appropriately score a response. Under these conditions, while all efforts should be made to complete the Rorschach, the examiner should make a decision as to whether under such a situation a valid protocol can in fact be obtained. Throughout the testing process, but especially during the inquiry phase, the examiner must remain aware of the special needs of adolescents. Adolescents will often structure the Rorschach experience similarly to how they present themselves and interact with others. The clinician knowledgeable about adolescents will be able to address some of the adolescent's presented needs without breaking Rorschach protocol, thus allowing for a valid assessment.

Being able to master interpretation of Rorschach protocols according to the Comprehensive System requires that the clinician be formally trained as well as an avid student of Exner's texts (Exner, 1986; Exner & Weiner, 1982; Exner, 1985). In interpreting Rorschach protocols for children and adoles-cents, Weiner (1986) maintains that the clinician must be aware that the Rorschach is "primarily a measure of perceptual–cognitive style in which the subject's problem solving approach reflects key dimensions of his or her psychological traits and states" (p. 144). In other words, we can draw some conclusions regarding the way a particular adolescent may approach other situations through analysis of Rorschach data. The ambiguity of the Rorschach presents the adolescent with a problem solving situation, necessitating that the youngster bring forth a sample of his or her own behavior (Weiner, 1986). The question then arises: with what degree of certainty can a clinician affirm that the behavior presented during the administration of the Rorschach is similar to behavior the adolescent will demonstrate outside the testing situation? If clinicians analyze how the adolescent approached the task (e.g., Did she or he use the entire blot area in organizing her or his percept, or was she or he stimulated by the color in the card in originating the percept?) as opposed to just looking for the presumed meaning behind the response, Exner (1986) and Weiner (1986) assert that their interpretation of Rorschach protocols can offer clinicians insight into the behaviors, coping mechanisms, and personality characteristics of the adolescent respondent.

There are special considerations in evaluating protocols of adolescent clients. Specifically, Weiner (1986) asserts that it is essential that the clinician be aware of three factors. First, clinicians need to be cognizant of "normative expectations" of adolescent behavior on the Rorschach (p. 149). For example, normal adolescents tend to offer whole responses less frequently than children. Additionally, normal adolescents tend to combine form and color — with form being primary — more often than children, who tend to give more color/form responses with color being more primary (Exner & Weiner, 1982). The Comprehensive System allows for comparison of individual adolescent Rorschach responses with a normative sample of adolescent Rorschach variables with a year-by-year age breakdown (Exner et al., 1985). Evaluating adolescent protocols therefore involves comparisons with same-age peers, thus decreasing any possible misapplications of the adult interpretive literature. By comparing individual protocols with normative data, the clinician has some empirical quidelines by which to judge aberrant responses.

Weiner (1986) also stipulates that interpretation of adolescent Rorschach protocols needs to be made within the context of knowledge of normal and pathological adolescent development. Rorschach variables obtained through scoring with the Comprehensive System are meaningful only to the degree that they can assist in characterizing the adolescent's current functioning and stipulating possible intervention strategies. Translating Rorschach data into a conceptualization of the adolescent's functioning necessitates that the examiner understand manifestations of normal and deviant behavior in adolescence. The Rorschach was not designed as a diagnostic instrument, with such disorders as depression, anxiety, and juvenile delinquency in mind. Therefore, clinicians need to be cognizant of characteristics of individuals displaying such symptomatology in evaluating adolescent Rorschach protocols (Weiner, 1986). The question the clinician assessing adolescents must answer in extrapolating personality characteristics, traits, and coping mechanisms from Rorschach data is how adolescents who present specific disorders would characteristically act on ambiguous tasks such as the Rorschach. For example, oppositional disordered youngsters tend to be noncompliant, defensive, self-centered, and angry. On the Rorschach this attitude may manifest itself in behaviors such as giving a low number of total responses, higher than average use of white space in organizing percepts, a high egocentricity index, and high preponderence of aggressive content.

Finally, Weiner (1986) also maintains that it is essential that the clinician be aware of issues related to fluidity and stability of personality in adolescents. While there are some personality variables which are relatively fixed early in life, the very nature of the developmental phase of adolescence includes a great deal of inner reorganization and change. Thus, in interpreting adolescent protocols it is imperative that the clinician remain sensitive to this potential for change when making predictions about future behavior (Weiner, 1986). However, adolescents in comparison with children, are to some degree more set in terms of personality dynamics, and consequently the clinician can make statements about some of the coping mechanisms which remain more stable. Toward this end, Exner (1983) has collected normative data on variables which remain consistent in test–retest trials with an adolescent population. It is through remaining close to empirical and normative data that the Comprehensive System offers great value in allowing clinicians to ascertain pertinent and useful information from adolescent Rorschach protocols.

PROJECTIVE DRAWINGS

There is currently a reemphasis on using projective drawings as diagnostic aids in the assessment process (Oster & Gould, 1987). Drawings provide the examiner with rich and valuable information when used as supplements to traditional psychological batteries and historical information. Their special value as projective instruments remains as "clinical tools" and as adjunctive interviewing devices in allowing the examiner to generate hypotheses regarding personality descriptions (Anastasi, 1982). Because of their brevity, nonthreatening nature, and ease of administration, drawings are an ideal way in which to initially engage adolescents in the assessment process and seem to be the most frequent adjunct to such commonly used projective techniques as the Rorschach and TAT.

Drawings for evaluative purposes may include "free drawings", where the task is left completely to the individual, or more "structured" drawings (e.g., "draw a person"), where specific instructions are provided by the examiner, who then judges the completed product based on theoretical orientation, previous research, normative data, and personal experiences. It is also helpful to elicit the examinee's interpretation of the drawings and to view them within the context of his or her developmental stage of life (Oster & Gould, 1987). With this information, the clinician can begin to form insight into the examinee's conceptual, intellectual, and emotional functioning.

John Buck (1948), Karen Machover (1952), Emanuel Hammer (1967), and Elizabeth Koppitz (1968) have been the main advocates of using figure drawings as projective instruments. When used in this manner, human figure drawings can be analyzed for the appearance of emotional indicators. The drawings are seen as a reflection of the individual's emotional conflicts and attitudes. These emotional indicators or signs can be grouped into three categories. One such grouping is the overall quality of the drawn figure. This relates to such aspects of the drawings as line quality (e.g., sketchy or broken), integration of body parts and their proportions, and shading. Another grouping of signs considers the specific features that are typically not seen in human drawings. These include items such as a large or small head, teeth, crossed eyes, and cut-off hands. The last category of emotional indicators to observe in a human figure drawing is composed of items that are usually expected to be seen. Such body parts as eyes, nose, feet, and neck are the norm in drawings completed by adolescents. Omissions of these details can be considered important clues to the presence of emotional conflicts or psychopathology.

Although, like most projective techniques, research concerning the interpretations of drawings has met with discrepant results, the impact of using drawings in the assessment of personality has been tremendous (Koppitz, 1968). This popularity in the use of drawings among clinicians has prompted the development of numerous variations in what is to be drawn. The instructions provided to the adolescent about what to draw can highlight certain areas of potential conflict which allude to family dynamics, various emotions, and unpleasant experiences, to name a few. Each directive offers the adolescent a novel experience. Therefore the examiner should ask for a number of drawings in order to gather a wide range of relevant information. The following tests are only a small portion of the possibilities in requesting drawings from adolescents.

Draw-A-Person

The Draw-A-Person (DAP) Test was created by Karen Machover from her experiences with the Goodenough technique ("Draw-A-Man Test", Goodenough, 1926) for assessing children's intellectual capacities (Machover, 1952). Although numerous projective drawings had been utilized in searching for important diagnostic clues, most attention had focused on drawings of the human figure to explore personality dynamics. Hypotheses were generated that the human figure drawing portrayed an unconscious projection of how the person actually perceived him or herself and were reflections

AA—H

of self-concept. For example, an emotion such as hostility seemed to be commonly projected onto human figure drawings by glaring eyes, bared teeth, sneering lips, or even weapons placed in the hands of the drawn person (Hammer, 1967). Poor reality testing was also indicated by drawings of bizarre facial features (e.g., animal faces on human figures) or depersonalized, empty facial expressions. Other aspects of personality commonly observed in human figure drawings included concerns regarding sexual identification, portrayals of dominant and inferior persons, and impulses towards rebelliousness and seductiveness.

The Draw-A-Person technique is introduced to the adolescent by instructing him or her to simply "draw a person," after paper and pencil are provided. This brief directive, however, is often met with many questions like "Do I make a stick figure or a whole person or what kind of person?" (Koppitz, 1968). These inquiries are usually best answered with a vague, general statement (e.g., "Make the drawing in any way that you would like"). If the person protests due to personal feelings of incompetence regarding drawings, a reassuring statement such as, "Just do your best," or "I am not interested in how well you draw; rather I am just interested in you drawing a person," or "Whatever you do is all right" will usually suffice. Upon completion of the initial drawing, the examinee is requested to construct a person of the opposite sex in an attempt to delineate sexual identification, an important area in adolescent development. Since the overwhelming majority of individuals draw their gender initially from this directive (Machover, 1952), a deviation from this approach would indicate further exploration.

There is consensus among proponents of human figure drawings that no direct relationship exists between any specific sign or emotional indicator and a definite personality or trait (Koppitz, 1968; Hammer, 1967; Machover, 1952). Many attempts at researching these variables have shown that anxieties, conflicts, or attitudes can be expressed by various means in different people at different points in time. Definitive personality descriptions therefore should not be made from a single sign; rather, the total drawing, as well as combinations of indicators, must always be considered in analyzing the drawing. Additionally, the drawing must be interpreted on the basis of age, maturation, social and cultural background, and relevant history of the individual. An example of an element in a drawing that should be interpreted with caution is sketchiness in the line quality, which is sometimes viewed as an emotional indicator of anxiety. Accordingly, this sketchiness appears to increase with age and is the norm for most adolescents, who almost always demonstrate some degree of anxiety (Koppitz, 1968).

Draw-A-Person-In-The-Rain

A particularly intriguing modification of the DAP is the Draw-A-Person-In-The-Rain. This simple addendum to the basic instruction of drawing a person has resulted in an impressive array of results (Oster & Gould, 1987). The originator of this variation on the DAP (Arnold Abrams or Abraham Amchin [cited in Hammer, 1967]), attempted to design a technique that offered a perception of the self when placed within a symbol of an environmental stressor, that is, the rain.

From our own experience, this procedure provides useful information to the examiner when a concern has been expressed regarding the person's ego strength. Such referral questions as: "How will this person respond to stressful circumstances?"; "What kind of personal resources does this person possess to cope with anxiety-provoking environments?"; "Is this person able to plan effectively in situations that might be considered anxiety-provoking?" are all indications to utilize this simple adaptation to the DAP.

Often those adolescents who perceive themselves as being helpless will construct a self-portrait of being "dumped upon" by illustrating a disheveled person in a downpour with no protective covering (Oster & Gould, 1987). This kind of drawing also appears to represent possible underlying feelings of minimal self-regard and unresolved dependency issues. Adolescents who do not feel overwhelmed by their surroundings and have greater personal resources will typically draw protective clothing or devices (e.g., an umbrella) and contended facial expressions. Those adolescents who seem to react unfavorably to minimal stressors will usually portray themselves as panic-stricken without a means of escape.

It is a standard practice to make comparisons between this drawing and other human figure drawings completed during the evaluation, as well as other responses within the test battery. For example, do indications from a drawing of a tendency to withdraw in interpersonal situations coincide with responses to the Rorschach or TAT which may indicate a passive style of interacting? Does a standard drawing of a person deteriorate when conditions of possible stress are overlayed? In this latter illustration, the examiner many want to know whether the adolescent has the ability to employ an adequate amount of coping skills to present a facade of adequate functioning. Is it only when confronted with external stress that underlying fears reveal themselves? Often a person's predisposition towards abnormal reactions is not visible in standard drawings. It is only when a novel request is made that the latency of any pathological dimensions are discovered, which, of course, is an important function of most projective evaluations.

Draw-A-Family

An elaboration on using human figure drawings as projective indicators of personality is The Draw-A-Family or Family Drawing Technique, initially suggested by Appel (1931) and later by Wolff (1942). Its popular use seems to parallel the modern therapeutic emphasis on family systems theory (Oster and Gould, 1987). The instructions direct the examinee to "draw a picture of your whole family" (Harris, 1963). If the adolescent does not spontaneously offer the names of family members, he or she is asked to identify them after the drawing is completed.

The primary use of the resulting drawings is to ascertain the outstanding features of the adolescent's perceived status within the family hierarchy. For instance, adolescents who view themselves as having greater significance in the family when compared to siblings will likely place themselves in greater proximity to the parents and make themselves as large as parental figures. In marked contrast, adolescents who feel isolated or different from their siblings might draw themselves off to one side or not participating in a family activity. It is sometimes seen that the examinee will omit him or herself from the family drawing entirely, which is usually a reflection of feelings of rejection. This is particularly demonstrated in family drawings by adopted children, especially during their adolescent years when identity concerns become focused (Di Leo, 1983).

A particularly useful modification to the family drawing is the Kinetic Family Drawing (KFD) (Burns & Kaufman, 1970), which adds the drawing directive, "Do something (an activity) together." In this variation, it is essential for the adolescent to include him- or herself and is usually given after the first, more general family drawing instruction so as not to forgo the possibility that the individual will omit him- or herself. This latter addition sometimes produce a reaction like, "We don't do anything together" (which is key information in the gathering of initial hypotheses regarding familial interaction with adolescents). At other times, adolescents will draw their families engaged in a very passive posture (e.g., watching television or a movie), which gives the examiner a clue to a possible lack of familial communication. Another common outcome when using the kinetic family drawing technique are pictures reflecting scenes at the dinner table. Here the adolescent may place the parents at opposite ends of a very long table (indicating a perceived emotional distance between the two) or may draw him or herself at one end (attesting to his or her need for greater status or in being a parentified child). Whether the dinner table is full or bare may address an adolescent's worries about living in a bleak environment or concerns regarding the lack of emotional nurturance.

Other factors to be ascertained from the drawings include trying to assess the dynamics between parent(s) and the remaining familial configuration.

Clues to these dynamics may include whether the adolescent omits siblings partially or entirely, indicating a symbolic means to eliminate competition, or whether the family is drawn in accurate proportions (i.e., making a child or adult much taller demonstrates perceived dominance or ineffectiveness). Another clinical sign to notice from the drawing is the various expressions of the parents, if they are apparent. Whether the adolescent perceives one or both parent(s) to be harsh, gentle, or supportive are all important areas to pursue during the remainder of the assessment to provide direction for future therapeutic planning.

Selecting A Drawing

The drawings that result from such common instructions as "Draw a House," "Draw a Tree," "Draw a (particular) Feeling," and "Draw your earliest recollection" offer the adolescent concrete expressions of his or her inner world. Because of the small amount of time examiners have to spend with adolescents, it becomes necessary to be well versed in the special advantages and disadvantages of each utilized drawing technique. Clinicians have increasingly incorporated a variety of drawing directives into their standard test batteries. Drawings provide, in a simple manner of administration, a richness of information lacking in other projective instruments. When drawings are interpreted in the context of other supporting information, examiners can provide thoughtful information to the referral sources which can aid in appropriate diagnosis and treatment.

THEMATIC APPERCEPTION TEST

The Thematic Apperception Test (TAT) is a popular projective technique developed by Henry Murray (1938) to help identify the important needs, emotions, and conflicts of the personality. In this test, a set of moderately ambiguous pictures are presented and the client is asked to make up stories about them.

As with other projective techniques, it is assumed that an individual will project aspects of his or her own personality when attempting to structure an ambiguous stimulus. It is further maintained that the strength of a particular psychological need or drive will be manifested in a discernible way in the individual's responses. Moreover, it is assumed that there is a meaningful relationship between an individual's responses on the test and important nontest behavior. In essence, the major underlying rationale of the TAT is that there is a relationship between the themes presented in the stories and the individual's current emotional functioning.

The absolute validity of these assumptions is not necessary for clinical use of the TAT. In fact, the projective hypothesis appears inadequate to account for all the responses given to an ambiguous stimulus. The instructions given to the client, the characteristics of the stimuli, the motivations of the client, and the client's subjective appraisal of the risks and benefits of different responses all help determine the final production. Likewise, there is not necessarily a direct relationship between projective responses and behavior in other situations. Indeed, thematic productions may represent a compensation for the lack of certain behavioral tendencies.

Responses to the TAT should be considered a sample of the client's thoughts, the significance of which must be determined within the context of all the relevant information available to the clinician. When used in this way, it can provide important hypotheses concerning the individual's view of the world, interpersonal relationships, relation to authority, and family dynamics. In addition, information about the client's needs, fears, motives, attitudes, and self-concept may be revealed. Moreover, the storytelling procedure provides the adolescent the opportunity to disclose in an indirect way issues and conflicts that he or she may be reluctant to discuss directly.

Although the instructions should be tailored to the developmental level of the client, the following instructions given by Murray (1943) for children are suitable for adolescents and, in fact, for most individuals:

> I have some pictures here that I am going to show you, and for each picture I want you to make up a story. Tell what has happened before and what is happening now. Say what the people are feeling and thinking and how the story will end. You can make up any kind of story you want. Do you understand? Well, then, here's the first picture (pp. 3–4).

The instructions can be repeated and modified as needed to aid in the understanding of the task.

It is very important to record the stories exactly as the client tells them. Many examiners use shorthand of some sort and others make an audio recording of the session and transcribe it at a later time. It is also worthwhile to make behavioral observations of how the adolescent reacts to the cards and to the stories as they are produced. For example, does the adolescent's speed of responding, tone of voice, or affect change when significant emotional themes are presented? Such changes may indicate areas of emotional conflict. Questions asked by the examiner should also be noted, so that the spontaneous productions of the adolescent can be kept separate from those elicited by the examiner's probing.

It is often necessary to prompt the adolescent to verbalize all the elements of a good story, including the present situation, preceding events, thoughts and feelings of the characters, and the outcome of the story. These prompts should be brief and to the point, for example, "How does it end?" or "Tell me their thoughts and feelings". If the client gives an especially brief response, the examiner may try to enrich it by asking "What happens next?". A more extensive inquiry should not be performed until after all the cards have been administered. This can have the purpose of clarifying the characters' motivations and actions or to investigate the source of the story without biasing the original responses.

Since television shows, fairy tales, and other forms of entertainment may form the basis of the story, it is often necessary to determine if this is the case or if the story was based primarily on personal experience. In this regard it may be helpful to ask "Is this story real?" or "What made you think of that story?". A story based on personal experience may hold greater significance for understanding the individual, but even stories based on popular culture may reveal important interests and attitudes.

There are 31 TAT cards, numbered so that a subset of 20 can be administered to one of four populations: males, females, boys, or girls. Cards with a number and the letter "M" were designed by Murray to be administered to males while a card and the letter "F", "B", and "G" were designed for females, boys, and girls respectively. Cards with a number and "GF" were for either girls or females, while a number and "BM" was for boys or males. Cards with just a number were to be used with everyone regardless of sex or age. One of the cards is blank and the client is asked to imagine a picture on it and make up a story about it. Theoretically, this allows for a greater amount of projection to occur, but the task is difficult for many adolescents and rather barren stories are often produced.

In contemporary clinical practice it is commonplace for eight to ten cards to be administered to a client as part of battery of tests (Goldstein & Hersen, 1984). The decision of which cards to use for a particular client is usually based on clinical judgment and is determined by the referral questions, as well as by the age and sex of the client. It is generally assumed that people will identify most closely with characters of the same sex and age, and consequently will produce richer and more meaningful responses to such cards. However, the clinician should feel free to select cards originally designed for any sex or age if the themes the card usually elicits will be relevant to an understanding of the individual.

In general, the following cards are recommended for use with adolescents: 1, 2, 4, 5, 7GF, 12F, 12M, 13MF, 15, 17BM, 18BM, 18GF. If the examiner has questions about the presence of depression or suicidal thoughts, then cards 3BM, 13B, 14, and 17GF may prove informative. Card 6BM, a card showing an elderly woman standing with her back toward a perplexed looking young man, may be helpful in revealing attitudes toward maternal figures. On the other hand, card 7BM, which shows an older man and a rather sullen younger man, has been useful in revealing attitudes toward authority and father figures, as has card 12M. Card 12M may also elicit feelings associated with the relationship between a client and therapist.

Although several scoring systems have been devised for the TAT, none has gained general use or demonstrated clear clinical utility. Normative data is lacking, and even in those systems where the scoring may be objective, the interpretation of the scores is still subjective. In actual clinical practice, the interpretation of TAT stories is usually subjective and qualitative rather than objective and quantitative.

Murray's ideas on the interpretation of the TAT are widely used even if his scoring system is not. The hero or heroes of the story are identified and their salient needs are noted. Needs are significant determinants of behavior that reside within an individual. They are inferred from the motives, behavioral trends, and feelings of the hero. The strength of a particular need is suggested by its intensity, duration, frequency, and general significance in the plots of the stories.

Murray identified numerous needs and inner states. Those of particular relevance to adolescents are the need for achievement, acquisition (i.e., to acquire things), affiliation, aggression, autonomy, excitance (i.e., to seek excitement), blame avoidance, rejection (i.e., to reject), recognition, and sex. Additional inner states such as conflict, sadness, distrust, moodiness, pride, elation, and jealousy should also be kept in mind when interpreting adolescent TAT stories.

In Murray's scoring system, the strength of each need was rated on a five-point scale for each story and summed over all the stories. Although this type of quantification is not commonly used, it is still helpful for the examiner to make some judgments about the relative strength of the various needs as revealed in the total record. It is also important to consider the extent to which needs are in conflict with each other or fuse together toward the same end. Does a strong need for affiliation conflict with a similarly strong need for aggression, and is some resolution of this conflict achieved? Does a need for autonomy support in some way a need for achievement, or does it inhibit achievement by finding its expression in negativism?

In addition to the needs and inner states of the hero, the examiner should also note the environmental forces acting upon the hero. Murray called these forces "press" and they may represent either objective aspects of the environment or the individual's perception of the environment. The hero may exist within a deprived, rejecting or hostile environment. He or she may be faced with coercion, imposed duty, injury, or death. On the other hand, the hero may experience friendship, help, and nurturance from the environment. An examination of these forces can reveal how the adolescent views the world in general and certain relationships (e.g., with parents) in particular.

The examiner should next consider the outcome of each story. In Murray's system, the interaction of the hero's needs, environmental press, and the outcome constitutes a simple *thema*. When evaluating a *thema*, it is important to assess the degree to which the hero is seen as an effective agent or a passive victim of circumstances. Does the hero overcome adversity through effort, or do successful outcomes have a magical quality? How are issues of right and wrong handled in the stories? Does the hero exhibit antisocial tendencies or excessive guilt? Is a moralistic outcome tacked onto the end of the story or implicit in it throughout? How does the hero deal with interpersonal relations and conflicts? Murray also suggested paying attention to the interests and sentiments attributed to the heroes of the stories, since these may shed light on the interests and attitudes of the subject.

It is also important for the examiner to evaluate the formal characteristics of the stories. Are the stories logical and well thought out, or do they reflect an impulsive cognitive style? Do the stories suggest good verbal expressive ability? Are there any indications of serious cognitive disorganization?

Although there are other projective thematic techniques applicable to adolescent populations, the Blacky Picture Test (Blum, 1950) and the Roberts Apperception Test for Children (McArthur & Roberts, 1982) being the most notable, the TAT enjoys the largest research base and widest popularity among clinicians. It is an easy and engaging task that lends itself to a variety of interpretive approaches. What it lacks in psychometric and normative qualities it makes up for in the richness of idiographic material. It provides a window on the unique needs, conflicts, interests, motivations, pressures, and coping styles of the individual adolescent client.

SENTENCE COMPLETION TESTS

Sentence completion tests are often described as an extension of the word-association method, and as such must be considered a semi-structured form of a projective technique. In this procedure, the examiner instructs the subject to read the beginning of a sentence, or stem, and to complete the remainder of the sentence. These sentence stems have been used in a variety of settings and with broad populations, but the task is generally the same; to add to a sentence stem in such a way as to produce a complete sentence that is typically indicative of a belief or attitude, or that conveys information about one's past or present experience. In employing this method with adolescents, it is assumed that their free associations will provide relevant diagnostic material.

In general, the introductory words, i.e., sentence stems, provide a practically unlimited variety of responses (Anastasi, 1982). Examples from these might include: What pains me . . . My father . . . What I enjoy . . . and so on. Many sentence stems are used to elicit from the examinee responses that seem relevant to his or her specific conflicts and concerns. This flexibility in its use makes it advantageous for the assessment of adolescents. Although, many standardized forms have been developed for adults there are several well-standardized versions for adolescents (e.g., Rotter, Rafferty, & Lotsoff, 1954; Rohde, 1957).

Probably the most frequently used sentence completion form for adolescents is the Rotter Incomplete Sentences Blank — High School Form (Rotter et al., 1954). Consisting of 40 sentence stems, the directions for this test are simple: "Complete these sentences to express *your real feelings*. Try to do every one. Be sure to make a complete sentence." Although many examiners use this form to derive projective hypotheses, an objective system has been created whereby each completed sentence is judged on a 7-point scale as to degree of adjustment versus maladjustment. The manual provides illustrations that correspond to each rating which are then summed to provide an overall adjustment rating that can be used for screening purposes. In addition to this process, individual responses can be examined clinically for specific diagnostic clues.

In selecting items for the various sentence completion tests, it seems that the main purpose has been to stimulate associations, often in specific content areas, in such a way as to overcome resistance (which is very relevant to the assessment of adolescents). Whereas Rotter was sensitive to one issue (i.e., degree of conflict), other sentence completion authors, most notably Rohde, ascribed to a broader purpose — with her test attempting to correspond to Murray's interacting need-press system (Palmer, 1983). Rohde was therefore less concerned with the stem structures than with the variability in responses. She has illustrated these response possibilities at length in the description of the way she developed her set of sentence stems (Rohde, 1957).

Both Rotter and Rohde have constructed well-standardized forms for adolescent populations. Whereas Rotter distinguishes his forms for adolescents and adults by content, Rohdes, whose test was standardized on a sample of ninth graders, uses the same test for both groups. Both authors have presented data illustrating good repeat and scorer reliability, as well as data to support their hypothesis that their tests distinguish between normal and abnormal youth. When used in an appropriate manner, Rotter's scoring system has the advantage of a single score, indicating degree of conflict, whereas Rohde's system has the potential for yielding a clinically richer set of personality variables.

Although the sentence completion tests have enjoyed popularity among clinicians in their ability to elicit a large variety of themes, examiners must realize that these tests may be neutralized by defensive adolescents who can easily assess the nature of the tests. It has been shown that a large variety of individuals often give sterotypical and ambiguous responses when completing the stems. This is particularly true of adolescents, who are often flippant in their approach to formalized testing. Although this attitude does indicate to the examiner some information about the adolescent's defiance of authority or level of anxiety, it does impede the examiner in his or her attempt to discover broader aspects of functioning.

In sum, sentence completions may be thought of as midway between a subjective report and the associative process. Adolescents are generally aware that the stems and directions are being provided to encourage associations. For the minimal time investment involved in completing this task, the sentence completion does provide a cost-effective approach in sampling many adolescent responses.

Chapter 10

Computerized Assessment

USES OF THE COMPUTER FOR PSYCHOLOGICAL TESTING

With the proliferation of available computer technology for the general public, psychologists are beginning to discover both the potential benefits and liabilities of automating psychological assessment procedures. In terms of the benefits of using computers in psychological assessment, computers have demonstrated some efficiency in the areas of administration, scoring of protocols, and tabulation of normed results.

Additionally, computers have been used in interpreting test data and in report generation. While these applications of computer technology have been gaining in popularity over the past decade, there has been and continues to be considerable resistance by psychologists to the use of the computer for psychological testing (Butcher, 1987a). Historically, the use of the computer in scoring and tabulation of normed results has presented the least cause for resistance and therefore has been more widely accepted. Additionally, the superhuman speed of the computer for performing tedious and complex tasks involved in some scoring procedures, as well as the elimination of the human error factor, have made use of the computer more attractive and valuable to psychologists. Despite these articulated benefits of automating the psychological testing process, a tremendous amount of controversy remains as to whether test administration, interpretation, and report writing should be delegated to a machine.

ADVANTAGES OF COMPUTERIZED ASSESSMENT

There are a number of advantages in using computers in psychological testing, including: (a) objectivity, (b) client's attitude, (c) cost effectiveness,

(d) time effectiveness, (e) reliability, and (f) enhanced test development (Butcher, 1987; Hofer & Green, 1985). With regard to objectivity, computers serve as a mechanism by which examiner bias can be curtailed, leading to a sophisticated improvement in the precision and accuracy of test adminis- tration, scoring, and interpretation (Butcher, 1987a). Specifically, computer- administrated tests can produce results unaffected by the clinician's subjec- tive feelings. Under the more traditional face-to-face interactions of the testing process, clients may react to any transmitted feelings on the part of the clinician, which in turn may effect such examinee behaviors as test-taking strategies, honesty in answering test items, and motivation to demonstrate his or her best performance. The computer eliminates any interpersonal transactions which could impact on the adolescent's performance. Computers are also potentially beneficial in increasing retest reliability and replicability, as the computer remains more consistent across time and testing sessions in terms of administration protocol and scoring procedures. The computer therefore eliminates the occasional "off day" even the best psychol- ogist will have. Additionally, computer-generated interpretation programs also eliminate examiner bias, as the same set of automated decision rules are applied to each individual (Butcher, 1987a).

Some clients may prefer the anonymity of having a test administered by a computer and may feel freer to answer questions honestly and completely (Hofer & Green, 1985). Use of computers in administering tests with an adolescent population may be extremely beneficial in terms of decreasing the self consciousness and guardedness which often typify adolescent interac- tions with examiners in the testing situation. Additionally, adolescents, who are part of the television-and-computer generation, may sustain greater attention and enhanced motivation when presented with a computer in contrast to the more mundane and perhaps more tedious process of complet- ing paper-and-pencil questionnaires. Additionally, with paper-and-pencil tests, the adolescent is usually presented with the entire test booklet and therefore from the very start is aware of the length of the particular test instrument. Assessment devices which are particularly long may cause the adolescent to adopt, from the very beginning, a more negative orientation to the examining process. With computerized assessment procedure, the length of the test is not always apparent, thereby decreasing the risk of the adolescent displaying this frustration (Hofer & Green, 1985). Finally, many adaptive devices are now available making true–false, multiple choice, and even voice responses possible for severely handicapped individuals, which gives these clients a sense of autonomy. Computer-generated voice can even make computerized testing available to adolescents who have difficulty with the reading level of the particular assessment instrument.

Although the initial purchasing or leasing of hardware and software may be expensive, it can be more cost effective to utilize the computer for administering and scoring psychological test protocols than to do so manually. Automated administration, scoring, tabulations of norms, and interpretation reduces the human time factor and associated salaries (Butcher, 1987). Consequently, psychological testing services can be dispensed in a timely manner, with costs to the consumer being potentially reduced due to the efficiency of the automation process.

With computers, test scores can be available within minutes instead of hours. Even if the psychologist decides not to purchase testing software but rather to utilize the services of a computer center, the use of the computer and modem still usually means a quicker return rate for test results. Specifically, complicated scoring procedures can be handled by computers with greater speed and accuracy, thereby freeing the clinician's time to pursue other endeavors (Butcher, 1987a). For example, electronic scanning and scoring of MMPI answer sheets allows clinicians to utilize numerous supplemental profiles, providing an added richness of interpretative data which would not have otherwise been possible without enormous effort. Additionally, many computerized assessment scoring programs also include normative data, which — for example — prints both the adolescent's scores and norms for the adolescent's same age peers, consequently saving the clinician the time of having to separately look up this information. Computers not only assist with efficiency in scoring testing protocols, but many computerized programs are available which contribute to greater efficiency in the subsequent *interpretation* of test data. Computer-generated interpretation of test scores may save the clinician the time spent having to consult various sources in order to obtain an accurate analysis of test results.

With the advent of advanced computer graphic capabilities, the development of new types of tests (e.g., using spatial abilities not available in paper and pencil formats) can be instigated. Additionally, measures of test-taking behaviors (e.g., response time) and test-taking strategies (e.g., observations regarding problem solving processes) are possible, thus freeing the examiner to make more specific observations (Hofer & Green, 1985). The computer also has the technical capability to improve on the selection of test items to present based on the statistical properties for a certain subject. This is accomplished by making split-second decisions regarding the appropriate avenue of questioning to pursue, based on the client's previous responses (Hofer & Green, 1985). The possible number of test items, as well as the time to administer them, can therefore potentially be reduced.

DISADVANTAGES OF COMPUTER-IZED ASSESSMENT

With so many advantages in using automated testing, it is a wonder that more psychologists haven't made extensive use of computers in their practice. While computer technology has been available to psychologists for some time, there is still a reluctance on the part of clinicians to accept computer administration, scoring, and especially interpretation of psychological tests. Of major concern is the idea that once their use was accepted, psychologists would put too much faith in automated processes, thereby limiting the practice of individually tailoring the assessment process. Critics of computerized testing have cited numerous disadvantages, including: (a) problems of equating computerized and paper-and-pencil versions of tests; (b) issues related to the excessively general nature of computer-generated interpretations; (c) the potential for misuse of computerized assessment protocols; (d) confidentiality; and (e) difficulties in maintaining quality control of computerized packages (Butcher, 1987a; Hofer & Green, 1985). By examining each one of these concerns, both the promise and limitations of computerized assessment can be more clearly delineated.

There are two central issues that need to be taken into consideration when paper-and-pencil tests are offered through a computerized format. First, the question arises as to whether the examinee's experience is equivalent in the paper-and-pencil version and the computerized form (Hofer & Green, 1985). In other words, are there any extraneous variables (e.g., motivation, test-taking attitude) which differentially impact on the examinee's test performance (Butcher, 1987a)? Hofer and Green (1985) present research which suggests that developers of computerized programs have underestimated the impact of computer-administered tests on performance. For example, persons not familiar with computers may exhibit some anxiety when asked to complete tests through an interactive process with a computer. Consequently, this situation-specific anxiety may effect test results in ways which might not occur if an individual was offered the more traditional paper-and-pencil format (Hofer & Green, 1985). Questions regarding test reliability center around concerns that norms and standards for interpretation based on paper-and-pencil administered tests are often applied to the computerized version without further validation studies (Hofer & Green, 1985).

Questions of reliability are also raised in terms of the equivalence of form and content between computerized and paper-and-pencil versions (Hofer & Green, 1985). Some of the advantages in using computer presentations of test items (e.g., making the individual focus more time on each question, keeping the individual from answering subsequent questions by referring to answers to previous questions) may alter the test responses enough to differ from the norms and standards established through development of the original paper-and-pencil format (Hofer & Green, 1985). While the above two complications of moving from a more traditional to computerized format do not call into question the usefulness of using computers, they do suggest that developers of computerized testing programs should make empirical comparisons between these two divergent formats to determine whether previously obtained norms and standards can be applied. In addition, research should be undertaken regarding the impact of extraneous variables on performance in computer-presented tests. This is especially important for adolescent and child populations, since most of the research to date deals only with adult subjects.

One of the major criticisms of computerized assessment centers on using computers to make interpretations of test results. While most clinicians may see the utility in allowing computers to handle the more mundane and tedious processes of administering and scoring responses, there is great debate as to the usefulness of relying on computers to make interpretations of test data. This is an especially sensitive issue, as it threatens the very nature of the psychologist's work. At best, the computerized interpretations are only valid as the available empirical research and the programmer's ability to simulate the interpretive process.

A central question is whether computer-generated interpretive statements can be useful to the individual case or whether they represent simplistic overgeneralizations which have limited utility for conceptualizing the person and developing treatment strategies tailored specifically for the individual (Butcher, 1987a). To some degree, anxiety surrounding interpretive computerized packages seems unfounded, since the computer can offer the clinician the same information that would be obtained from some other source in order to interpret test results. The clinician has the responsibility not to accept blindly the material presented, whether in a text or a computerized printout, and to choose instead only those interpretations which are valid for the particular client. The computerized interpretive statements are only overgeneralizations to the degree that the clinician does not accept responsibility for filtering out inappropriate material. The computer does not invalidate the clinician's important role in interpreting test data; rather, it can offer the clinician a valuable and efficient tool, by being a library for actuarial data and clinical insight. It is important, however, for computer programs to clearly delineate and document the source of the interpretive statements, so the clinician can know which interpretations are based on normative and actuarial data and which are derived from clinical theory (Hofer & Green, 1985). Toward this end, Hofer and Green (1985) and Butcher (1987a) suggest that problems in overgeneralizability of computerized interpretive statements would be severely curtailed if clinicians treated actuarial data differently than clinical insight, with clinically generated statements being more cautiously used.

Concerns over blanket acceptance of computer-generated interpretive statements have also fueled controversy in another area. Specifically, computerized assessment programs open up a new area for potential abuse and misuse of psychological test data (Butcher, 1987a). Although in the hands of well-trained, licensed psychologists, automated assessment programs can be a valuable tool, in untrained hands they can do more harm than good. This question applies to administration and scoring as well as interpretation.

It must be remembered that a computer-printed profile is not a psychological assessment. The output of any computer assessment must be interpreted in terms of the individual adolescent by a qualified psychologist. Of particular concern is the process of dissemination of information from the computer-generated profile. With so many psychological reports being introduced into the legal arena, it is important that computerized programs are not misrepresented. There is great pressure, especially within the judicial system, to find the "absolute science" in psychology; therefore, there is also great potential for abuse of the results obtained through computerized packages. The clinician must be extremely cautious about making statements that cannot be related to research data or clinical theory. The psychologist must also be very careful in the storing of computer-generated profiles (Butcher, 1987a; Hofer & Green, 1985). Access to the computerized report by untrained professionals can be quite dangerous, since a qualified psychologist is needed to make adequate translations from the computerized report to actual valid statements about the specific individual.

There is also concern about the potential abuse of computerized programs given the widespread availability of testing software to non-psychologists or psychologists without proper and sufficient training. In general, computer software can be purchased by anyone. Without control over who purchases and uses the psychological testing software, the test could be used incorrectly or put to wholesale use. Subsequently, there is justifiable concern that in untrained hands these test scores and interpretations — having been administered, scored, interpreted, and produced by a computer — will be unquestionably accepted as valid and infallible.

Another criticism of computerized assessment programs concerns issues related to confidentiality. Numerous computerized testing programs require that test responses be either sent by mail or telephone lines to commercial testing companies. While these are considered professional-to-professional communications and individual clients are assigned an identification number in order to mask their identity, it still involves sending intimate client data out of the office (Butcher, 1987b). Computer programs used within the confines of the individual practitioner's office also present problems for the maintenance of confidentiality. Specifically, computer scoring systems often store the data from many clients on a single disk. Therefore, if unauthorized access to the disk was obtained, the confidentiality of many individuals could be potentially violated. In order to guard against such terrible exposures, extra care should be instigated to secure computer records.

A final salient criticism of computerized assessment programs involves issues related to quality assurance (Butcher, 1987a). For the most part, computerized testing programs are available through commercial companies. Their interest in making a profit may be in direct conflict with concerns of clearly validating programs before they are available for marketing, ethical principles of confidentiality, and limiting access to the programs to licensed and qualified psychologists. The potential for abuse of computerized programs within the marketplace is high, since those interested in turning a profit may not wait for rigorous empirical research to be completed nor be willing to provide the capital base necessary for this research to be undertaken. Therefore, it is imperative that the individual psychologist fully analyze the theoretical and research underpinnings of available computer programs before utilizing them in his or her practice, as the ethical responsibility for properly administering, scoring, and interpreting test data remains with the clinician, no matter what tools — computer or otherwise — are employed in the process.

ETHICAL PRINCIPLES IN THE USE OF COMPUTERIZED ASSESSMENT

In order to establish some standards for the development and use of computerized assessment programs, the American Psychological Association (APA) has recently adopted new guidelines for computerized assessment (Guidelines for Computer-Based Tests and Interpretations, APA, 1986). The stated purpose of these guidelines (which are advisory in nature) are "to assist professionals in applying computer assessments competently and in the best interests of their clients" and to "guide test developers in establishing and maintaining the quality of new products" (Guidelines for Computer-Based Tests and Interpretations, APA, 1986, p. 2). These guidelines identify the specific ethical principles (Ethical Principles; APA, 1981), test standards (Testing Standard; APA, 1985), and service providers standards (Provider Standards; APA, 1977) applicable to issues raised by computerized assessment programs and delineate specific guidelines not covered in previously presented literature by the APA. The problem with these standards is that they only serve as governing rules to members of the APA. Thus, if commercial establishments choose not to follow these guidelines there is little recourse for trying to prevent inadequate computerized programs from being marketed. Perhaps the only power the APA has in this direction is to educate its members, forcefully explain to testing companies the value of following these guidelines for presenting reputable materials, and mobilizing its membership to financially boycott noncomplying companies and influence practitioners outside APA membership.

COMPUTER TECHNOLOGY IN THE
ASSESSMENT PROCESS

There are a variety of different modes by which computers can be utilized in administering, scoring, or interpreting psychological tests. Computer-administered tests are only beginning to become more widely used, especially with regard to tedious self-report inventories (e.g., Minnesota Multiphasic Inventory or Personality Inventory for Children), interview schedules (e.g., Diagnostic Interview for Children and Adolescents) and neuropsychological assessment (Golden, 1987; Lachar, 1987; Stein, 1987). Specifically, computerized administration involves the adolescent in direct interaction with a terminal as questions are presented on the computer monitor, and the adolescent is subsequently instructed to select a response.

Historically, computer scoring of test data has been one of the earliest uses of computer technology in the field of psychological testing (Fowler, 1985). There are a variety of different mechanisms by which test protocols can be computer scored, including central processing, teleprocessing, and local processing (Moreland, 1987). Central processing involves sending test proto-cols through the mail to a central location where the data is scored and returned to the clinician. The biggest advantage of central processing is the limited expense, since it requires no investment in computer hardware or software and thus allows psychologists with a limited testing practice access to computer technology. Disadvantages of central processing includes the long waiting period between when test data is actually obtained and when the scored protocol is returned and the potential for a breach in confidentiality should the protocol be misfiled or lost in the mailing process. Despite these limitations, central processing is often the mode of choice for clinicians interested in beginning to experiment with the uses of computer technology for their practice.

With the decrease in the cost of microcomputers, teleprocessing and local processing have engendered increased popularity among psychologists (Moreland, 1987). Teleprocessing involves sending test data over the tele-phone wires through the use of a modem which connects a microcomputer with the computers (usually mainframe computers) at the central processing location. The advantage of teleprocessing over central processing is primar-ily the increased speed with which protocols can be scored and made available to the psychologist. This is an improvement in turnaround time from days to minutes. Local processing usually entails commercially avail-able scoring software which can be used by many available microcomputers, thus allowing the clinician to score protocols in the privacy of his or her office. While this has many advantages, including increased protection of records and greater flexibility in time management for the clinician, the cost of purchasing these computer programs may be extensive and prove taxing for the clinician just starting a practice. In addition, many databases in computer testing programs are quite extensive, and some scoring procedures for certain psychological test instruments may be very complicated; these programs may therefore not be adaptable to microcomputers. In that case, the clinician who is interested in extensively automating his or her assessment services may in reality have to combine local processing with either teleprocessing or central processing programs.

Mechanisms for interpretation of test protocols are available through the same three formats: central processing, teleprocessing, and microprocessing. Types of computerized interpretive programs vary widely, from those that just offer the individual's scores with actuarial data or developmental norms (e.g., RSCORE) to those programs which include narrative reports based on obtained test scores (e.g., RIAP). Some computer-generated interpretive packages (e.g., the MMPI Interpretive System — comprehensive 3.0) can be interfaced with word processing programs, thus allowing the psychologist the opportunity to more efficiently compose and edit test reports.

RECOMMENDATIONS

Using computers in psychological assessment offers psychologists relief from some of the tedious processes involved in administration and scoring of test data. For adolescent populations, the computer may also offer a more intrinsically motivating mechanism, thus perhaps increasing motivation and attention to various assessment instruments. The computer also has the potential to allow the psychologist to measure more accurately additional test behaviors, including reaction time, problem-solving strategies, and changes in physiological states. Computerized interpretive programs allow for increased access to a great wealth of actuarial and normative data, as well as clinical theory. Additionally, computers can continuously update data banks, thereby allowing for greater dissemination of more current normative data, research, and clinical conceptualizations. Not only are we still involved in uncovering further uses of computers in psychological testing, as well as refining current applications of computer technology, but we are also discovering the increased potential for abuse of computers within the field.

In using computers in psychological testing, it is absolutely essential that the psychologist remain responsible to the needs and concerns of the individual client. Computerized programs should only be used by qualified psychologists who have received adequate training. Within this context, many researchers involved in the development of computerized testing programs (e.g., Butcher, 1987a; Exner, 1987; Fowler, 1985; Hofer & Green, 1985) strongly assert that any computer-generated statement should be carefully scrutinized and evaluated for its validity, given relevant patient data, before the information is utilized in the psychological report. In the final analysis, any computer-generated testing programs are only as accurate as the normative data, empirical research, and clinical theory underlying specific test instruments (Exner, 1987). It therefore continues to be the responsibility of the individual clinician to evaluate the reliability and validity of any assessment instrument before using it to draw conclusions concerning the psychological functioning of a particular client.

Chapter 11

Writing The Psychological Report

The psychological report is the culmination of a process that begins with the referral questions and ends with an integration of the material gathered through interviewing, test administration, and other procedures, such as a review of the records and behavioral observations (Gabel, Oster, & Butnik, 1986). This report should present in a clear and concise manner information that will best aid those working with the adolescent, whether it be physicians, school officials, probation officers, or therapists. Each segment of the report should contribute to detailing the adolescent's personal resources and response styles and demonstrate how these personal and interpersonal attributes and limitations interact within his or her situation.

The length, specifics, and format of the psychological report will vary depending on the referral source, reasons for the assessment, questions that need to be clarified, types of instruments administered, and the writing style of the psychologist. Additional information that may not have been included in the report (e.g., informal discussions with parents) may be communicated verbally or placed in a cover letter to the person making the referral. It is crucial to determine what material needs to be included and what is the best way to convey that information. Since adolescents are in a number of interacting subsystems (e.g., family, school, social agencies) and all of which may have access to the report. The usual problems encountered in selecting and organizing information for the report are magnified in the assessment of adolescents.

WHAT TO INCLUDE IN A REPORT

What is necessary for a final report is best determined by the questions asked by the referral source. These questions, besides providing a framework for interviewing and test selection, will aid in determining which relevant

122

facts and impressions to include in the report. There are also a number of general points to consider when deciding what needs to be included. Although not a comprehensive list, the following outline may help in determining the scope of the report:

- Clearly answer each referral question.
- If the report is going to help in determining placement, then make recommendations and include the relevant data to support your conclusions.
- Identify the factors that may be affecting the growth and development of this individual.
- Eliminate psychological jargon. Write to your audience.
- Describe the adolescent's performance in a manner relating to his or her general interpersonal and academic efficiency.
- Include raw data or verbatim material only if you are trying to support your hypotheses.
- Statements surrounding your degree of certainty about the test data should not be too tentative or overly generalized. If you have to doubt your own conclusions they will be of little benefit to other professionals. Any interpretive statements you make should stand up to peer review.
- Your recommendations should be comprehensive enough to ensure that the adolescent you have evaluated will receive all the possible services available.

SECTIONS OF THE PSYCHOLOGI-CAL REPORT

There are usually several discrete but interrelated areas that are in the formal presentation of the evaluation. These include the following sections, which will be found in most reports, although the headings may differ:

- Identifying information
- Reasons for referral
- Previous evaluations
- Instruments included in the present examination
- Historical data and/or knowledge gained from interviewing the youth and family
- Behavioral observations
- Test results and interpretations
- Summary and conclusions
- Recommendations

Identifying information

This initial part of the psychological report describes the relevant demographic information pertaining to the adolescent. It usually contains the youth's name, address, birthdate and age, educational level, and the name of the school he or she is currently attending. This section may also include such additional facts as the date(s) of the evaluation and the name of the referral source.

Reasons for referral

This paragraph attempts to delineate the reasons for performing an evaluation on this particular youth. As discussed more thoroughly in chapter 1, the reasons for referral are central to the evaluation and interpretation of the results. It is helpful to cover all the questions that are being asked in this section, as they will provide a framework for the conclusions and recommendations. This section usually covers the presenting problems that the adolescent is experiencing and the events that precipitated the referral source being involved.

Previous evaluations

The following portion reports on whether previous evaluations have been performed and how recent these have been. (Many times a referral will come in for an intellectual assessment when the youth has just been given a WISC-R at a different agency within the past month!). A listing of numerical data from these reports is especially helpful, in order to provide a basis of comparison to the present results. A summary of the important conclusions also indicates what treatment interventions have been considered or implemented in the past.

Instruments included in the present evaluation

This segment lists the assortment of test instruments used in the present evaluation. Numerical results can also be placed in this section for ease of reading instead of, or in addition to, including them in the body of the report. By placing the scores in this section, the reader can easily compare these to the previous section on prior testing. Results of projective tests, such as the Rorschach or TAT, are usually integrated into the other sections of the report and are seldom presented in a numerical manner. Although there are different opinions on this matter, it is our view that the advantages of including numerical results often outweigh the concern regarding the possible misinterpretation of these data. For example, it may be hard for the reader to follow your reasoning behind suggesting that an individual may have a learning disability based on the scattering of his or her scores without listing the exact variability. Moreover, certain sophisticated readers, such as special education teachers, may find the raw data particularly helpful in understanding the adolescent's learning style. If the same report is to be sent to a number of different individuals, some of whom will benefit from the numerical results, these scores can be placed in an addendum and attached to those specified reports.

Background information

The next part in the report usually describes the pertinent historical data based on previous reports and interviews of the adolescent and his or her family. Information derived from these sources usually includes the developmental history, elaborations on the precipitating events that led to the referral, family constellation and dynamics, current stressors, and the social context. Much of this knowledge can be derived from a careful interview of the youth and family (See chapters 2, 3 and 4), which can lead to hypotheses about the problems being presented. It is important to include information that will help the reader understand the conclusions and recommendations.

Behavioral observations

The direct observation of behavior during the testing session provides an abundance of information about the adolescent's emotional, social, and cognitive functioning. The examiner should get in the habit of closely watching the adolescent's behavior during the session and making detailed notes either during the session itself or immediately afterward. In particular, the examiner should comment on the individual's physical appearance, level of cooperation, activity level, attention span, impulsivity, distractibility, frustration tolerance, overall mood, emotional reactivity, anxiety level, motivation to perform, quality of verbal communication, attitude toward the examiner, and variability of behavior over time. In addition, any handicapping conditions of the individual or limitations of the setting that may have affected the testing administration should be mentioned. It is sometimes helpful, especially for the beginning examiner, to use a cue card with the above areas delineated, to aid in a comprehensive description of the examinee's behavior when writing the report.

It is also important for the examiner to arrive at a conclusion regarding the representativeness of the individual's current level of functioning. Factors such as motivation and cooperation need to be considered when making this determination. In general, a factor that appears situationally determined (e.g., resentment at being tested) may threaten the integrity of the findings, while factors reflecting more stable personality characteristics (e.g., impulsivity) may not. It is helpful in this regard for the examiner to be observant of changes in the examinee's behavior over the course of the session. For example, if the adolescent's level of anxiety subsides considerably through-

AA—I*

out the session, then its possible inhibitory effect on the initial parts of the evaluation should be acknowledged as a factor that may have influenced some of the scores. However, if the examinee remains highly anxious throughout the session, despite attempts to make him or her comfortable, then the inhibitory effects of that anxiety may interfere with functioning in a wide range of situations, and no qualifying statements about the validity of test results would be necessary.

Test results and interpretations

An integration and synthesis of the test results and the possible implications that these results have on the functioning of the individual are central to this section of the test report. In describing the test results in relation to the youth's cognitive and emotional status, the examiner is providing a framework for the understanding of many different aspects of the youth's abilities and shortcomings. This allows the referral source the opportunity to appreciate more fully the resources the adolescent possesses, and helps him or her in formulating the treatment strategies that may be most effective.

The initial part of this section usually presents a summary of the adolescent's intellectual functioning. It would typically include IQ scores and an explanation of their meaning in relation to the individual adolescent. Many report writers find it useful to mention the range in which the Full Scale IQ falls and the percentile rank that this represents for the examinee. Some mention of the scatter or range of scores, in relation to the individual or standardized norms for a particular age group, is also helpful to the reader (Sattler, 1982). Additionally, a summary statement indicating whether the examiner affirmed that the scores were representative of the adolescent's true abilities and reflect his or her everyday functioning level (e.g., distractibility or anxiety interfering with accurate knowledge of questions) can aid the reader in planning intervention strategies.

In reporting the actual scaled scores or a summary of these scores, it is important to detail the kinds of skills reflected by the various subtests given to the adolescent, and how his or her strengths or weaknesses in these areas will impact on his or her everyday functioning. For example, if there is a significant discrepancy between the Verbal and Performance scales, or weaknesses on the scales associated with sustained attention, these should be delineated and discussed in relation to hypotheses concerning the adolescent's learning style and possible difficulties he or she may experience in the classroom or work environment. If a more comprehensive battery of tests was given for organic impairment or learning deficits (e.g., Halstead-Reitan) the results would also be provided in this section in a similar manner.

Closely related to intellectual functioning and its relationship to other areas of skills or deficits are the topics of perceptual–motor maturation and accumulated achievement. This supportive information can assist the examiner in reaching a conclusion about specialized weaknesses or possible learning disabilities. For instance, poor performance on the Bender-Gestalt test, when combined with lowered scores on certain intellectual subscales tapping similar abilities, would suggest a dysfunction in this important area and the need for awareness of this limitation in planning treatment interventions. Furthermore, an estimate of achievement (e.g., as reflected by the WRAT-R) can give additional information as to current level of functioning.

Following this summary on what skills a particular adolescent possesses in order to comprehend the world, a section of the report is devoted to how the adolescent evaluates the world affectively. This section could focus on personality traits and how these traits impact on interpersonal relationships; or on how they may create problems for the adolescent; or may be organized around central conflicts or problems related to the referral questions. Usually, the examiner needs to gain information regarding what factors of the adolescent's reality testing or perceptual style may impede everyday functioning and to assess the degree or severity of this possible disturbance. The examiner also needs to highlight the salient themes that occur throughout the adolescent's responses, as related to his or her emotional concerns and conflicts. Other areas that need to be addressed in this section typically include the adolescent's level of impulse control, degree of depressive thoughts or feelings, major defenses, needs for attention, potential for acting out conflicts, and other underlying feelings relating to self-image (Houck & Hansen, 1972; Levy, 1963).

A concluding summary statement in this section of the psychological report addresses the adolescent's ability to relate intimately to others. This is particularly important in addressing the need for and desired type of psychotherapeutic intervention. An emphasis on the area of interpersonal functioning is crucial if effective treatment is to take place. Such questions as (a) Will this individual benefit from an insight oriented approach to psychotherapy or will he or she respond more effectively to behaviorally-oriented interventions?; (b) Are the adolescent's main struggles centered around familial conflicts, therefore indicating a family therapy recommendation?; (c) Are there specific conflicts (e.g., sexual difficulties) that need to be focused on during treatment?; and (d) Is the reluctance to share with others or to trust figures in authority going to interfere with a psychotherapeutic relationship? — all need to be shared with the referral source and other readers of the report. Other personality traits describing overall maturity level, ability to verbalize thoughts and feelings, projected compliance with treatment, and general social skills would all be topics for discussion in planning intervention strategies (Tallent, 1976). Finally, a general statement regarding the adolescent's potential for violence, either directed at self or others, should be included, especially in reports for juvenile justice or hospital officials.

Summary and conclusions

A final narrative section attempts to combine the various discrete "parts" of the report, into a relevant and coherent whole. This is the time for the psychologist to offer diagnostic impressions and provide suggestions for interventions based on the experience of being with the adolescent. In specifying well-reasoned hypotheses concerning the case, the psychologist should consider what in the adolescent's environment is maintaining the problematic behaviors. This integration of test findings with the adolescent's background information helps in portraying a complete picture of the adolescent to the referral source and provides a basis for individualized treatment.

Often this section becomes the most vital in planning treatment for the adolescent, since it is assumed that the statements made in this section are based on all the preceding data and information. It is often the only section read or reported. Therefore, it is important to reiterate the outstanding aspects of the interview and test results into a well-conceptualized statement of the adolescent's strengths, weaknesses, and needs. It is essential that the description of the adolescent is accurate, pertinent, and useful to the referral source.

Recommendations

The concluding portion of the report includes a list of discrete recommendations regarding what the psychologist suggests would further benefit the adolescent and his or her situation. Although the referral questions are the basis for the organization of the section, additional information is often requested in the form of providing optimal choices for intervention based on the uniqueness of the adolescent and his or her own life situation. In providing this information, the examiner should attempt to address each inference made in the test interpretation part of the report. For example, if the adolescent's functioning is evaluated and explained in terms of cognitive, emotional, interpersonal strengths and weaknesses, then the recommendations should attempt to provide ways in which the adolescent would be able to live more effectively — in school, at work, and with his or her family and friends (van Reken, 1981).

When working with adolescents, the issue of placement outside of the home becomes a familiar and important question, one that needs to be addressed within this section. In discussing this question, the psychologist is usually required to discuss the degree of structure necessary to permit effective functioning for a particular youth and the extent that the youth is a danger to himself or others. Thus, the psychologist should be aware of the available options in out-of-home placement, if this is warranted, and whether this placement needs to be short or long term and whether a locked facility is needed.

Another important area of concern included in this list is to what degree therapeutic intervention is required and what approaches would be most effective. In most circumstances, especially in inpatient settings, a variety of treatment modalities are available (e.g., individual, group, expressive, psychodrama) and these should be mentioned if indicated from the evaluation. The availability of the parents for family therapy needs to be addressed, including what mode of family intervention would most likely have the best results.

Since this section should be as specific and comprehensive as possible, any additional evaluations (e.g., educational or neurological assessments) need to be explicitly mentioned. Also, the availability of the examiner for followup contacts, in coordinating treatment interventions or reevaluations, needs to be detailed. The examiner should keep in mind that psychological reports are often kept in a permanent file and follow the adolescent in some form or another throughout his or her life. Thus, the report should be constructed in a positive and helpful manner.

Chapter 12

Explaining the Evaluation Results to the Family

There are instances in which clinicians will be requested, mainly by the family of the adolescent being assessed, to explain the results of the psychological evaluation. This request may stem from the family's lack of understanding when, for instance, they were provided with only parts of the report at a larger conference on the adolescent (e.g., at a school conference or juvenile court hearing), or when they have received the results second-hand, for instance, in the office of the pediatrician who made the assessment referral. It is also possible that the family was too nervous to understand all that was said at the time of first delivery, and wants to carefully review all aspects of the evaluation in greater detail (Gabel, Oster, & Butnik, 1986).

IMPORTANCE OF THE FEEDBACK

Whatever the reason, clinicians must always expect and be prepared for these requests for information. In fact, from our own experience, the informing interview should always be an integral part of the assessment process. It emphasizes the value of the evaluation, provides the adolescent and family with an opportunity to gain some perspective on the presenting problems, and gives them a chance to clarify all questions they may have concerning their current situation. It also allows the family the opportunity to explore alternative services that may be available to them and to receive some elaboration on the recommendations. Most importantly, when framed in a positive and supportive manner, it allows the adolescent to hear why he or she may have been experiencing personal, interpersonal, or academically related problems and what appropriate intervention may be available to him or her.

The informing interview consists of several aspects and is part educational, part motivational, and part therapeutic. Technical information must be conveyed regarding the adolescent's intellectual and emotional strengths and weaknesses and how these interact with his or her present circumstances. For clinicians, this means that the presentation must be both knowledgeable and thorough, and must reflect sensitivity to the best interests of the youth and family. This is true whether the adolescent being assessed is being charged with severe delinquent activities, is suicidal, or has minor learning difficulties.

MAKING AN EFFECTIVE DELIVERY

It is important to stress that successful informing interviews do occur. Although there may be several contributing external factors that impede the quality of information delivered or received (e.g., the degree of sophistication of the parents or child, prior experience with professionals, anger or embarrassment about the precipitating events), there are certain techniques the psychologist can use to minimize some of these problems. It is important to use language that is understandable to all those present in the interview. Because of the differences in developmental levels and varying differences in education, it is usually best to eliminate all psychological jargon and attempt to reduce unnecessary technical nuances of the results. In presenting the results, it is often necessary to repeat much of the information until it is established that everyone understands what is being communicated. It is also essential to reflect back to the family their concerns. Empathy and supportive statements are always the best allies! A clear, concise delivery which focuses on the positive aspects of the youth and family, emphasizes the major findings of the assessment, and leaves plenty of time for questions is often the best strategy.

It is important to make the reporting of specific results understandable for everyone in the room. For instance, instead of reporting specific scores of an IQ test, it is better to present the results as a comparison to other, same-grade-level peers, with emphasis on the strengths. If reporting a possible learning disability, it is helpful to have available a number of daily examples where this specific cognitive deficit may be hampering the adolescent's daily functioning. An example would be informing the youth and her parents that since Joan experiences difficulty in auditory sequencing, it may be beneficial for her to use other sensory modalities, such as visual cues, as a compensatory strategy. When offering results of personality test it is sometimes helpful to use analogies that portray a clearer picture of the adolescent's problems. For instance, one might describe defense mechanisms in the context of an offensive line in football, where a breakdown in performance of one of the players (e.g., the guard position) has caused difficulty in successfully running a play. Another tactic is to discuss a problem along with an intervention strategy for the family to use. An example would be to introduce the idea of a cooling off period, if, according to the psychological profile, the youth overreacts to minor irritants or has a poorly developed tolerance for frustration.

Clinicians must anticipate a variety of emotional reactions to the information being delivered and must be prepared to respond accordingly. The clinician should not go into the informing interview thinking that the material presented will only be experienced cognitively. Acknowledging the feelings that are being expressed allows the family to know that they are being heard and understood on several levels. In this manner, they are likely to appreciate the respect that is being given to them. Individuals respond best to those professionals who convey, through their demeanor and actions, an aptitude for listening to what is being said, an understanding of individual and family concerns, and an appreciation for the emotional messages being interchanged. It is also valuable to plan the interview in such a way as to allow the time and flexibility required to get to know the adolescent and family within a personal framework.

INTERVIEW FORMAT

Introductory statements

After some brief introductory remarks, the clinician should begin the session by asking the parents to state their primary concerns and the information they hope to gain from the evaluation. This allows the clinician to hear the referral questions from the parents' point of view in order to tailor the feedback to their major concerns. The clinician may follow up on this information by asking the parents and the adolescent what they think the causes of the problems are, and what they think should be done about them. This additional questioning enables the clinician to gauge: their understanding of the problems, the language used in describing the problems, and any resistance they may have to the information the clinician is about to present. It is a common mistake for beginning clinicians to rush into an explanation of test findings without first assessing the parents' willingness and ability to accept the results and recommendations.

It is also helpful to make a statement at the beginning of the session about the interest and caring the parents have demonstrated by their investment of time and energy in the assessment process. Moreover, the clinician should mention at the beginning several positive qualities of the youth who was tested, to set a positive tone for the proceedings and to reassure the parents that they are not totally incompetent or failures as parents.

Explaining the problems in nontechnical terms

It is important to use language that all family members can understand, so jargon and overly technical terms should be avoided. When it is necessary to use a technical term, it should be fully explained in non-technical language when first introduced. If the clinician was successful in eliciting the parents' views on the problem, then he or she should have some idea as to the level they can receive and understand information. Misconceptions of the problems should be addressed within the parents' existing conceptual framework as much as possible. For example, if the father explains his son's academic problems as the result of "fear of failure", while the evaluation indicates the presence of a specific learning disability, then the evaluator should explain how the youth's learning handicap may lead to these types of fears and, in turn, may lower his son's motivation and confidence. By integrating the new information within the parents' existing conceptual framework, the clinician makes the findings easier for the parents to both understand and accept.

The technique of asking the parents pertinent questions can be used throughout the informing interview. For example, if a learning disability in math has been detected, it would be helpful to ask if any other member of the immediate or extended family has or has had this problem, and how they were able to compensate for this interference in their learning. Since it is likely that others in the family have experienced a similar problem, a discussion is likely to ensue regarding not only the symptoms but also the frustrations and other concomitant feelings involved in having a handicapping condition. This approach allows the family to join with the adolescent on a level of togetherness, as opposed to isolation. This approach can also be used to introduce information about intellectual functioning and how the adolescent compares with other, same age peers. This presents an opportunity for the family to hear that other children may have similar problems, and to learn what resources might be available to them in order to follow up on the evaluation.

Supporting evidence for diagnosing the problem

At this stage of the interview, the clinician may begin to detail more of the assessment process. An elaboration of the various instruments provided to the adolescent and why they were chosen may be explained. In discussing IQ tests, for example, the clinician may introduce the concept of ranges and what it may mean for the adolescent to be within a particular range. It may be helpful to use diagrams or charts to illustrate certain points. When addressing the uses of the personality instruments, the clinician will want to emphasize to the family, as he or she did to the adolescent, that there were no right or wrong answers but that each and every person has a unique way of responding to the Rorschach, for example, and that unique way was the information the examiner needed to formulate hypotheses concerning how the youth reacts to and interprets his or her world.

It should be noted that the use of labels or technical diagnoses will most assuredly produce emotional reactions. Providing information on how a learning disability or an emotional disturbance may impact on the individual and the family is helpful, but only if it is done in a simple, straightforward context which attempts to demystify misunderstood terms. The introduction of this material should also be done in a therapeutic manner, with emphasis on supportive statements and plans for intervention. The clinician should be prepared to offer specific recommendations to the family on how to deal with the problems they are facing. These recommendations should be clearly related to the previously presented findings, and presented in a way that will minimize resistance. The clinician should not avoid making unpopular recommendations, however, and should leave sufficient time to explore questions and concerns the parents might raise.

Making sure that all questions have been pursued

It is helpful to formulate at the end of the interview all questions that have been asked, and address those that may have been overlooked by the family, but are usual sources of misunderstanding. In providing a framework for this review, the clinician may want to explicitly state some unspoken concerns of the family, such as: "Who else will have access to this information?" "What degree of structure does the adolescent require to meet all his or her needs, and can the family provide for this?" "What should the family anticipate concerning their involvement if the adolescent is hospitalized or placed outside of the family?" By making these questions overt, many of the family's fears and feelings of guilt can be minimized. Many practical questions can be discussed and additional contacts for consultation can be arranged. This is especially important if an evaluation for medication is being discussed or additional tests for physical problems are being recommended.

In covering these unasked questions, it may be helpful to explore with the family their worry about the future. A statement such as, "It seems as though you are wondering whether your son will ever be able to become independent" may allow the parents to elaborate on their fears. Another, more indirect avenue is to acknowledge that many parents have this general concern about their children and that it produces many self-doubts about their child-rearing practices. It may be helpful to pursue this line of questioning with the parents alone, as these issues may lead to the admission of conflicts in the marriage that need to be explored without the involvement of the children. Discussion without the child present also provides the parents with a forum to more freely express their personal fears regarding the future.

Final remarks

Final clarification of all major points needs to be undertaken at this time. The adolescent and family should be offered the opportunity to raise any final questions, and each should be asked individually about their understanding of what has been discussed throughout the session. Any disagreements should be reviewed thoroughly, and confusions clarified. Any future contact should be planned and any appointments for further information sharing or counseling scheduled. If the evaluation was completed at the request of the parents, they should be complimented for acting on their concerns and encouraged to pursue the strategies and recommendations that have been discussed. This respect for the concern of the family should also be provided even if the evaluation was requested from a third party. Such respect increases the likelihood that the parents will continue pursuing effective treatment for their child.

References

Achenbach, T. M. (1966). The classification of children's psychiatric symptoms: A factor analytic study. *Psychological Monographs, 80.*

Achenbach, T. M., and Edelbrock, C. S. (1978). The classification of child psychopathology: A review and analysis of empirical efforts. *Psychological Bulletin, 85,* 1275–1301.

Achenbach, T. M., and Edelbrock, C. S. (1983). *Manual for the child behavior checklist and revised child behavior profile.* Burlington, VT: Thomas M. Achenbach.

American Psychological Association. (1977). *Standards for providers of psychological services.* Washington, DC: Author.

American Psychological Association. (1985). *Standards for educational and psychological testing.* Washington, DC: Author.

American Psychological Association. (1986). *American Psychological guidelines for computer-based tests and interpretation.* Washington, DC: Author.

American Psychological Association. (1981). Ethical principles of psychologists. *American Psychologist, 36(6),* 633–638.

Anastasi, A. (1982). *Psychological Testing.* New York: Macmillan.

Appel, K. E. (1931). Drawings by children as aids in personality studies. *American Journal of Orthopsychiatry, 1,* 129–144.

Archer, R. P. (1984). Use of the MMPI with adolescents: A review of salient issues. *Clinical Psychology Review, 4,* 241–251.

Archer, R. P. (1987). *Using the MMPI with adolescents.* Hillsdale, NJ: Lawrence Erlbaum.

Barron, F. (1953). An ego strength scale which predicts response to psychotherapy. *Journal of Consulting Psychology, 17,* 327–333.

Beck, S. J. (1981). Reality, Rorschach, and perceptual theory. In A. I. Rabin (Ed.), *Assessment with projective techniques* (pp. 23–46). New York: Springer Publishing Company.

Bender, L. (1938). A visual motor gestalt test and its clinical use. *American Orthopsychiatric Association Research Monographs,* No. 3.

Benton, A. L. (1974). *The Revised Visual Retention Test* (4th ed.). New York: Psychological Corporation.

Berg, E. A. (1948). A simple objective test for measuring flexibility in thinking. *Journal of General Psychology, 39,* 15–22.

Berger, M. (1976). Psychological testing. In M. Rutter and L. Herson (Eds.), *Child and adolescent psychiatry: Modern approaches.* London: Blackwell Scientific Publications.

Blos, P. (1962). *On adolescence.* New York: Free Press.

Blotcky, A. D. (1984). A framework for assessing the psychologic functioning of adolescents.

Developmental and Behavioral Pediatrics, 5, 74–77.

Blum, G. S. (1950). *The Blacky Pictures: Manual of instructions.* New York: Psychological Corporation.

Brown, D. T. (1985). Review of Millon Adolescent Personality Inventory. In J. V. Mitchell (Ed.), *Ninth mental measurement yearbook, vol. 1, pp. 978–979.* Nebraska: Buros Institute of Mental Measurement.

Buck, J. N. (1948). The H-T-P test. *Journal of Clinical Psychology, 4,* 151–159.

Burns, R. C., and Kaufman, S. H. (1970). *Kinetic family drawings (K-F-D): An introduction to understanding children through kinetic drawing.* New York: Brunner/Mazel.

Butcher, J. N. (1985). Why MMPI sort forms should not be used for clinical predictions. In J. N. Butcher and J. R. Graham (eds.), *Clinical applications of the MMPI* (pp. 10–11). Minneapolis: University of Minnesota Department of Conferences.

Butcher, J. N. (1987a). Computerized clinical and personality assessment using the MMPI. In J. N. Butcher (Ed.), *Computerized psychological assessment* (pp. 3–14). New York: Basic.

Butcher, J. N. (1987b). The use of computers in psychological assessment: An overview of practices and issues. In J. N. Butcher (Ed.), *Computerized psychological assessment* (pp. 161–197). New York: Basic.

Centofanti, C. C. (1975). *Selected somatosensory and cognitive test performances as a function of age and education in normal and neurologically abnormal adults.* (Doctoral dissertation, University of Michigan) Dissertation Abstracts International, 36, 3027B.

Centofanti, C. C., and Smith, A. (1979). *The Single and Double Simultaneous Stimulation Test Manual.* Los Angeles: Western Psychological Services.

Christensen, A. L. (1975). *Luria's neuropsychological investigation.* New York: Spectrum.

Costa, L. D., Vaughan, H. G., Levita, E., and Farber, N. (1963). Purdue Pegboard as a predictor of the presence and laterality of cerebral lesions. *Journal of Consulting Psychology, 27,* 133–137.

Cowan, T. A. (1963). Decision theory in law, science and technology. *Science, 140,* 1065–1075.

Cronbach, L. J. (1970). *Essentials of psychological testing.* New York: Harper's International Edition.

Dahlstrom, W. G., Welsh, G. S., and Dahlstrom, L. E. (1972). *An MMPI handbook: Vol. 1. Clinical interpretation.* Minneapolis, MN: University of Minnesota Press.

Denes, F., Semenza, C., and Stoppa, E. (1978). Selective improvement by unilateral brain-damaged patients on Raven Coloured Progressive Matrices. *Neuropsychologia, 16,* 749–752.

Derogatis, L. R. (1977). *SCL-90-R (revised version).* USA: Author.

Di Leo, J. H. (1983). *Interpreting children's drawings.* New York: Brunner/Mazel.

Dunn, L. M. (1974). *Manual for the Peabody Picture Vocabulary Test-Revised.* Minneapolis, MN: American Guidance Service.

Dunn, L. M., and Dunn, L. M. (1981). *Peabody Picture Vocabulary Test-Revised.* Circle Pines, MN: American Guidance Services.

Dunn, L. M., and Markwardt, L. C., Jr. (1970). *The Peabody Individual Achievement Test.* Circle Pines, MN: American Guidance Services.

Duthie, B. (1985). *Manual for the Adolescent Multiphasic Personality Inventory.* Richland, WA: Pacific Psychological.

Erikson, E. H. (1968). *Identity: Youth and crisis.* New York: W. W. Norton.

Evans, I. M., and Nelson, R. O. (1977). Assessment of child behavior problems. In A. R. Ciminero, K. S. Callhoun, and H. E. Adams (Eds.), *Handbook of behavioral assessment.* New York: Wiley-Interscience.

Exner, J. E. (1974). *The Rorschach: A comprehensive system. Volume 1.* New York: Wiley.

Exner, J. E. (1983). Rorschach Assessment. In I. B. Weiner (Ed.), *Clinical methods in psychology* (2nd Ed.) (pp. 332–347). New York: Wiley.

Exner, J. E. (1985). *A Rorschach workbook for the comprehensive system* (2nd Ed.). Bayville, NY: Rorschach Workshops.

Exner, J. E. (1986). *The Rorschach: A comprehensive system. Volume 1. Basic foundations.* New York: John Wiley & Sons, Inc.

Exner, J. T. (1987). Computerized assistance in Rorschach interpretation. In J. N. Butcher (Ed.), *Computerized psychological assessment* (pp. 218–235). New York: Basic.

Exner, J. T., and Weiner, I. B. (1982). *The Rorschach: A comprehensive system. Volume 3: Assessment of children and adolescents.* New York: Wiley.

Finch, S. M., and Green, J. M. (1979). Personality disorders. In J. Norsitz (Ed.), *Basic handbook of child psychiatry: vol. 2.* New York: Basic.

Fish, B. and Ritvo, E. R. (1979). Psychosis of childhood. In J. Nospitz (Ed.), *Basic handbook of child psychiatry: vol. 2.* New York: Basic.

Fowler, R. D. (1985). Landmarks in computer-assisted psychological assessments. *Journal of Consulting and Clinical Psychology, 53(6),* 748–759.

Gabel, S., Oster, G. D., and Butnik, S. M. (1986). *Understanding psychological testing in children: A guide for health professionals.* New York: Plenum Medical.

Gleser, G., Seligman, R., Winget, C., and Rauh, J. L. (1977). Adolescents view their mental health. *Journal of Youth and Adolescence, 6,* 249–263.

Goldberg, T. E., and Smith, A. (1976). *Revised criteria for Purdue Pegboard neuropsychodiagnostic applications.* Unpublished manuscript, University of Michigan Medical School.

Golden, C. J. (1987). Computers in neuropsychology. In J. N. Butcher (Ed.), *Computerized psychological assessment* (pp. 218–235). New York: Basic.

Golden, C. J., Hammeke, T. A., and Purisch, A. D. (1980). *Manual for the Luria–Nebraska Neuropsychological Battery.* Los Angeles: Western Psychological Services.

Golden, C. J., Hammeke, T., and Purisch, A. D. (1978). Diagnostic validity of a standardized neuropsychological battery derived from Luria's neuropsychological tests. *Journal of Consulting and Clinical Psychology, 46,* 1258–1265.

Golden, C. J., Sawicki, R. F., and Franzen, M. D. (1984). Test construction. In G. Goldstein and M. Hersen (Eds), *Handbook of psychological assessment.* New York: Pergamon.

Goldman, J., Stein, C. L., and Guerry, S. (1983). *Psychological methods of child assessment.* New York: Brunner-Mazel.

Goldstein, G., and Hersen, M. (1984). *Handbook of psychological assessment.* New York: Pergamon.

Goodenough, F. L. (1926). *Measurement of intelligence by drawings.* New York: Harcourt, Brace, and World.

Gottesman, I. I., and Fishman, D. B. (1961). *Adolescent psychometric personality: A phonotypic psychosis.* Paper presented at the meeting of the American Psychological Association.

Graham, J. R. (1977). *The MMPI: A practical guide.* New York: Oxford University Press.

Greene, R. L. (1980). *The MMPI: An interpretive manual.* New York: Grune and Stratten.

Groth-Marnat, G. (1984). *Handbook of psychological assessment.* New York: Van Nostrand Reinhold.

Gutkin, T. B. (1978). Some useful statistics for the interpretation of the WISC-R. *Journal of Consulting and Clinical Psychology, 46,* 1, 561–563.

Haley, J. (1973). *Uncommon therapy: The psychiatric techniques of Milton H. Erickson.* New York: Norton.

Haley, J. (1980). *Leaving home: The therapy of disturbed young people.* New York: McGraw-Hill.

Hale, R. L. (1983). Intellectual assessment. In M. Hersen, A. E. Kazdin, and A. S. Bellack (Eds.), *The clinical psychology handbook.* New York: Pergamon Press.

Hammeke, T. A., Golden, C. J., and Purisch, A. D. (1978). A standardized, short, and comprehensive neuropsychological test battery based on the Luria neuropsychological evaluation. *International Journal of Neuroscience, 8*, 135–141.

Hammer, E. F. (1967). *Clinical applications of projective drawings.* Springfield, IL: Charles C. Thomas.

Harkaway, J. E. (Ed.) (1987). *Eating disorders.* Rockville, MD: Aspen.

Harris, D. B. (1963). *Children's drawings as measures of intellectual maturity.* New York: Harcourt, Brace, and World.

Hartlage, L. C. and Telzrou, C. F. (1983). The neuropsychological bases of educational intervention. *Journal of Learning Disabilities, 16*, 521–528.

Hartlage, L. C., and Telzrow, C. F. (1986). *Neuropsychological assessment and intervention with children and adolescents.* Sarasota, FL: Professional Resource Exchange.

Hathaway, S. R., and McKinley, J. C. (1967). *Minnesota Multiphasic Personality Inventory manual (revised).* New York: Psychological Corporation.

Hathaway, S. R., and Monachesi, E. D. (1963). *Adolescent personality and behavior.* Minneapolis, MN: University of Minnesota Press.

Heaton, R. K. (1981). *Wisconsin card sorting test manual.* Odessa, FL: Psychological Assessment Resources.

Hirshoren, A., and Kavale, K. (1976). Profile analysis of the WISC-R: A continuing malpractice. *The Exceptional Child, 23*, 83–87.

Hofer, P. J., and Green, B. F. (1985). The challenge of competence and creativity in computerized psychological testing. *Journal of Consulting and Clinical Psychology, 53(6)*, 826–839.

Hoffman, N. G., and Butcher, J. N. (1975). Clinical limitations of MMPI short forms. *Journal of Consulting and Clinical Psychology, 43*, 32–39.

Houck, J. E., and Hansen, J. C. (1972). Diagnostic interviewing. In R. H. Woody and J. D. Woody (Eds.), *Clinical assessment in counseling and psychotherapy.* Englewood Cliffs, NJ: Prentice-Hall.

Jastak, S., and Wilkinson, G. S. (1984). *Wide Range Achievement Test-Revised.* Wilmington, DE: Jastak Associates.

Jesness, C. F. (1962). *The Jesness Inventory: Development and validation (Research Rep. No. 29).* Sacramento, CA: California Youth Authority.

Jesness, C. F. (1963). *Redevelopment and revalidation of the Jesness Inventory (Research Rep. No. 35).* Sacramento, CA: California Youth Authority.

Jesness, C. F. (1983). *The Jesness Inventory Manual* (rev. ed.). Palo Alto, CA: Consulting Psychologists Press.

Jesness, C. F. and Wedge, R. F. (1983) *Classifying offenders: Classification system technical manual.* Sacramento, CA: California Youth Program, Research and Review Division.

Kanun, C. and Monachesi, E. D. (1960). Delinquency and the validating scales of the MMPI. *Journal of Criminal Law, Criminology and Police Science, 50*, 525–534.

Kaufman, A. S. (1979). Factor Structure of the WISC-R at 11 age levels between 6½ and 16½ years. *Journal of Consulting and Clinical Psychology, 43*, 133–147.

Kaufman, A. S. (1975). *Intelligence testing with the WISC-R.* New York: Wiley.

Keyser, D. J., and Sweetland, R. C. (1984). *Test Critiques (Vol. 1).* Missouri: Test Corporation of America.

Koppitz, E. M. (1968). *Psychological evaluation of children's human figure drawings.* New York: Grune and Stratton.

Lachar, D. (1987). Automated assessment of child and adolescent personality: The Personality Inventory for Children (PIC). In J. N. Butcher (Ed.), *Computerized psychological assessment.* New York: Basic.

Lachar, D., and Gdowski, C. L. (1979). *Acturial assessment of child and adolescent personality:*

An interpretive guide for the Personality Inventory for Children profiles. Los Angeles: Western Psychological Services.

Lachar, D., Butkus, M., and Hryhorczuk, L. (1978). Objective personality assessment in children: An interpretive guide for the Personality Inventory for children (PIC) in a child psychiatry setting. *Journal of Personality Assessment, 42,* 529–537.

Levine, D. (1981). Why and when to test: The social context of psychological testing. In A. I. Rabin (Ed.). *Assessment with projective techniques.* New York: Springer.

Levy, L. H. (1963). *Psychological interpretation.* New York: Holt, Rinehart, and Winston.

Lezak, M. D. (1983). *Neuropsychological assessment* (2nd ed.). New York: Oxford University Press.

Loader, P., Burck, C., Kinston, W., and Bentovim, A. (1982). A method for organizing the clinical description of family interaction: The family interaction summary format. In F. W. Kaslow (Ed.), *International book of family therapy.* New York: Brunner/Mazel.

Lueger, R. J. (1983). The use of the MMPI-168 with delinquent adolescents. *Journal of Clinical Psychology, 39,* 139–141.

MacAndrew, C. (1979). On the possibility of psychometric detection of persons prone to the abuse of alcohol and other substances. *Addictive Behaviors, 4,* 11–20.

Macbeth, L., and Cadow, B. (1984). Utility of the MMPI-168 with adolescents. *Journal of Clinical Psychology, 40,* 142–148.

Machover, K. (1952). *Personality projection in the drawing of the human figure.* Springfield, IL: Charles C. Thomas.

Madanes, C. (1986). Outline for case study. Unpublished manuscript. Family Therapy Institute of Washington, D.C., Rockville, MD.

Marks, P. A., Seeman, W., and Haller, D. (1974). *The actuarial use of the MMPI with adolescents and adults.* Baltimore, MD: Williams and Wilkens.

Matarazzo, J. D. (1972). *Wechsler's measurement and appraisal of adult intelligence* (5th ed.). New York: Oxford University Press.

McArthur, D. S., and Roberts, G. E. (1982). *Roberts Apperception Test for Children: Manual.* Los Angeles: Western Psychological Services.

McCarthy, J. J., and McCarthy, J. F. (1969). *Learning disabilities.* Boston: Allyn and Bacon.

McGoldrick, M., and Gerson, R. (1985). *Genograms in family assessment.* New York: W. W. Norton and Company, Inc.

Meeks, J. E. (1979). Behavioral and antisocial disorders. In J. Nospitz (Ed.), *Basic handbook of child psychiatry: Vol. 2.* New York: Basic.

Millon, T. (1969). *Modern psychopathology.* Philadelphia, PA: Saunders.

Millon, T. (1981). *Disorders of personality: DMS-III – Axis II.* New York: Wiley – Interscience.

Millon, T., Green, C. J., and Meagher, R. B., Jr. (1977). *Millon Adolescent Personality Inventory.* Minneapolis, MN: National Computer Systems, Inc.

Minuchin, S. (1974). *Families and family therapy.* Cambridge, MA; Harvard University Press.

Mishne, J. M. (1986). *Clinical work with adolescents.* New York: Free Press.

Moreland, K. L. (1987). Computerized psychological assessment: What's available. In J. N. Butcher (Ed.), *Computerized psychological assessment* (pp. 26–49). New York: Basic.

Murray, H. A. (1938). *Explorations in personality.* New York: Oxford University Press.

Murray, H. A. (1943). *Manual of Thematic Apperception Test.* Cambridge, MA: Harvard University Press.

Myers, P. I., and Hammill, D. D. (1969). *Methods for learning disorders.* New York: Wiley.

Newmark, C. S., and Thibodeau, J. R. (1979). Interpretive accuracy and empirical validity of abbreviated forms of the MMPI with hospitalized adolescents. In C. S. Newmark (Ed.), *MMPI: Clinical and research trends,* (pp. 248–275). New York: Praeger.

Offer, D. (1969). *The psychological world of the teenager.* New York: Basic.

Oster, G. D. and Gould, P. (1987). *Using drawings in assessment and therapy: A guide for mental health professionals.* New York: Brunner/Mazel.

Purdue Research Foundation (1948). *Purdue Pegboard.* Chicago: Science Research Associates.

Purisch, A., Golden, C. J., and Hammeke, T. (1978). Discrimination between schizophrenics and brain-damaged patients using the Luria-Nebraska Neuropsychological Battery. *Journal of Consulting and Clinical Psychology, 46,* 1266–1273.

Quay, H. C. (1964). Personality dimensions in delinquent males as inferred from the factor analysis of behavior ratings. *Journal of Research in Crime and Delinquency, 1,* 33–37.

Quay, H. C., Morse, W. C., and Cutler, R. L. (1966). Personality patterns of pupils in special classes for the emotionally disturbed. *Exceptional Children, 32,* 297–301.

Raven, J. C. (no date). Guide to the Standard Progressive Matrices. London: H. K. Lewis, 1960; New York: Psychological Corporation.

Raven, J. C. (1965). Guide to using the Coloured Progressive Matrices. London: H. K. Lewis.

Redl, F., and Wineman, D. (1951). *Children who hate.* Glencoe, IL: Free Press.

Rey, A. (1964). *L'examen Cliniue en psychologie.* Paris: Presses Universitaties de France.

Rohde, A. R. (1957). *The sentence completion method: Its diagnostic and clinical application to mental disorders.* New York: Ronald.

Rorschach, H. (1942). *Psychodiagnostics.* Bern: Verlag Hans Huber.

Rosenthal, R. H., and Akiskal, H. S. (1985). Mental status examination. In M. Hersen and S. M. Turner (Eds.), *Diagnostic interviewing* (pp. 25–52). New York: Plenum Press.

Rotter, J. B., Rafferty, J. E., and Lotsof, A. B. (1954). The validity of the Rotter Incomplete Sentences Blank, High School Form. *Journal of Consulting Psychology, 18,* 105–111.

Saffer, J. B., and Kelly, G. L. (1974). Treating the obese adolescent. *The Psychiatric Forum, 4,* 27–32.

Sattler, J. M. (1972). *Assessment of children's intelligence.* Philadelphia: Sanders.

Sattler, J. M. (1982). *Assessment of children's intelligence and special abilities.* Boston: Allyn and Bacon.

Siassi, I. (1984). Psychiatric interviews and mental status examinations. In G. Goldstein and M. Hersen (Eds.), *Handbook of psychological assessment* (pp. 259–275). New York: Pergamon.

Smith, A. (1973). *Symbol Digit Modalities Test.* Los Angeles: Western Psychological Services.

Spiers, P. A. (1981). Have they come to praise Luria or to bury him? The Luria-Nebraska controversy. *Journal of Consulting and Clinical Psychology, 49,* 331–341.

Spitzer, R. L., and Williams, J. B. W. (Eds.) (1987). *Diagnostic and statistical manual of mental disorders.* Washington, DC: American Psychiatric Association.

Stanley, J. C. (1971). Reliability. In R. L. Thordike (Ed.), *Educational measurement.* Washington, DC: American Counsel on Education.

Stein, M. D., and Davis, J. K. (Eds.) (1982). *Therapies for adolescents.* San Francisco: Jossey-Bass.

Stein, S. J. (1987). Computerized-assisted diagnosis for children and adolescents. In J. N. Butcher (Ed.), *Computerized psychological assessment* (pp. 145–160). New York: Basic.

Stewart, M. A. (1980). Personality and psychoneurotic disorders. In S. Gabel and M. T. Erickson (Eds.), *Child development and developmental disabilities.* Boston: Little, Brown.

Stierlin, H., Rucker-Embden, I., Wetzel, N., and Wirsching, M. (1980). *The first interview with the family.* New York: Brunner/Mazel.

Sundberg, N. D. (1977). *Assessment of persons.* Englewood Cliffs, NJ: Prentice-Hall.

Tallent, N. (1976). *Psychological report writing.* Englewood Cliffs, NJ: Prentice-Hall.

Taylor, E. M. (1959). *The appraisal of children with cerebral deficits.* Cambridge, MA; Harvard University Press.

van Reken, M. K. (1981). Psychological assessment and report writing. In C. Eugene Walker (Ed.), *Clinical practice of psychology.* New York: Pergamon.

Vincent, K. R. (1984). Diagnostic Inventory of Personality and Symptoms (DIPS): A new test of psychopathology based on DSM-III. *The Journal of Houston International Hospital, 3,* 1,

20-27.

Voelker, S. L. (1979). *Nethylphenidate in the treatment of hyperactivity in children: Prediction of short-term responses and multi-source assessment of long-term effects on behavior and academic achievement.* Unpublished doctoral dissertation, Wayne State University.

Watzlawick, P. (1984). *The invented reality.* New York: Norton.

Wechsler, D. (1958). *The measurement and appraisal of adult intelligence* (4th ed.). Baltimore, MD: Williams and Wilkins.

Wechsler, D. (1974). *WISC-R manual: Wechsler Intelligence Scale for Children — Revised.* New York: Psychological Corporation.

Weiner, I. B. (1980). Psychopathology in adolescence. In J. Aselson (Ed.), *Handbook of adolescent psychology.* New York: Wiley.

Weiner, I. B. (1986). Assessment with the Rorschach. In H. M. Knoff (Ed.), *The assessment of child and adolescent personality.* New York: Guilford.

Weins, A. N., and Matarazzo, J. D. (1983). Diagnostic interviewing. In M. Hersen, A. E. Kazdin, and A. S. Bellack (Eds.), *The clinical psychology handbook* (pp. 309-328). New York: Pergamon.

Welsh, G. S. (1956). Factor Dimensions A and R. In G. S. Welsh and W. G. Dahlstrom (Eds.), *Basic reading on the MMPI in psychology and medicine.* Minneapolis, MN: University of Minnesota.

Widiger, T. A. (1985). Review of Millon Adolescent Personality Inventory. In J. V. Mitchell (Ed.), *Ninth mental measurement yearbook (Vol. 1)* (pp. 979-981). Nebraska: Buros Institute of Mental Measurement.

Williams, C. L. (1985). Use of the MMPI with adolescents. In J. N. Butcher and J. R. Graham (Eds.), *Clinical applications of the MMPI* (pp. 37-39). Minneapolis, MN: University of Minnesota Department of Conferences.

Wilson, D. R., and Prentice-Dunn, S. (1981). Rating scales in the assessment of child behavior. *Journal of Child Clinical Psychology, 10,* 121-125.

Wirt, R. D., Lachar, D., Klinedinst, J. K., and Seat, P. D. (1977). *Multidimensional description of child personality: A manual for the Personality Inventory for Children.* Los Angeles: Western Psychological Services.

Wolff, W. (1942). Projective methods for personality analysis of expressive behavior in preschool children. *Character and Personality, 10,* 309-330.

Woodcock, R. W., and Johnson, M. B. (1977). *Woodcock-Johnson Psycho-Educational Battery, Part II: Tests of Achievement.* Boston, MA: Teaching Resources Corporation.

Author Index

143

Subject Index

147

About the Authors

Gerald D. Oster, PhD, is Director of Psychology Internship Training and a primary therapist at the Regional Institute for Children and Adolescents in Rockville, MD and is a licensed psychologist in private practice. He is co-author of *Understanding Psychological Testing in Children* (1986), *Using Drawings in Assessment and Therapy* (1987), *Difficult Moments in Child Psychotherapy* (1988) and *Overcoming Adolescent Depression* (1989).

Janice E. Caro, PhD, serves as primary therapist, psychological examiner on the court evaluation unit, and intern supervisor at RICA. She is also a licensed psychologist in private practice specializing in child, adolescent, and family therapy, and is co-author of *Overcoming Adolescent Depression* (1989).

Daniel R. Eagen, PhD, serves as primary therapist, intern supervisor, and director of research and evaluation at RICA. He is a licensed psychologist with specialized interests in neuropsychological assessment, cognitive–behavioral therapy, and program evaluation.

Margaret A. Lillo, MA, CCC-A, is a licensed audiologist specializing in hearing and information processing evaluations, both at RICA and in private practice. She is also a computer programmer, chairs the computer assessment committee, and supervises audiology graduate students at RICA.

RICA is a State and County supported, community-based day and residential treatment center and school for 180 seriously emotionally disturbed youths, aged 6–20. Having admitted its first children in 1980, it is now fully accredited by the Joint Commission on Accreditation Of Hospitals (JCAH). RICA is highly committed to the training of doctoral interns in psychology and students in other disciplines.

Psychology Practitioner Guidebooks

Editors
Arnold P. Goldstein, Syracuse University
Leonard Krasner, Stanford University & SUNY at Stony Brook
Sol. L. Garfield, Washington University in St. Louis

Elsie M. Pinkston & Nathan L. Linsk — CARE OF THE ELDERLY: A Family Approach

Donald Meichenbaum — STRESS INOCULATION TRAINING

Sebastiano Santostefano — COGNITIVE CONTROL THERAPY WITH CHILDREN AND ADOLESCENTS

Lillie Weiss, Melanie Katzman & Sharlene Wolchik — TREATING BULIMIA: A Psychoeducational Approach

Edward B. Blanchard & Frank Andrasik — MANAGEMENT OF CHRONIC HEADACHES: A Psychological Approach

Raymond G. Romanczyk — CLINICAL UTILIZATION OF MICRO-COMPUTER TECHNOLOGY

Philip H. Bornstein & Marcy T. Bornstein — MARITAL THERAPY: A Behavioral-Communications Approach

Michael T. Nietzel & Ronald C. Dillehay — PSYCHOLOGICAL CONSULTATION IN THE COURTROOM

Elizabeth B. Yost, Larry E. Beutler, M. Anne Corbishley & James R. Allender

SICALLY AND SEXUALLY ABUSED CHILD: Evaluation and Treatment

Robert E. Becker, Richard G. Heimberg & Alan S. Bellack — SOCIAL SKILLS TRAINING TREATMENT FOR DEPRESSION

Richard F. Dangel & Richard A. Polster — TEACHING CHILD MANAGE-MENT SKILLS

Albert Ellis, John F. McInerney, Raymond DiGiuseppe & Raymond Yeager — RATIONAL-EMOTIVE THERAPY WITH ALCOHOLICS AND SUB-STANCE ABUSERS

Johnny L. Matson & Thomas H. Ollendick — ENHANCING CHILDREN'S SOCIAL SKILLS: Assessment and Training

Edward B. Blanchard, John E. Martin & Patricia M. Dubbert — NON-DRUG TREATMENTS FOR ESSENTIAL HYPERTENSION

Samuel M. Turner & Deborah C. Beidel — TREATING OBSESSIVE-COMPULSIVE DISORDER

Alice W. Pope, Susan M. McHale & W. Edward Craighead — SELF-ESTEEM ENHANCEMENT WITH CHILDREN AND ADOLESCENTS

Jean E. Rhodes & Leonard A. Jason — PREVENTING SUBSTANCE ABUSE AMONG CHILDREN AND ADOLESCENTS

Gerald D. Oster, Janice E. Caro, Daniel R. Eagen & Margaret A. Lillo — ASSESSING ADOLESCENTS